Dream Inspiration in Books

How Best Selling Authors Interpreted Their Nightmares for Ideas in the Creative Writing Process

Victor Nyx

© **Copyright Victor Nyx 2025 - All rights reserved.**

The content within this book may not be reproduced, duplicated or transmitted without direct written permission from the author or the publisher.

Under no circumstances will any blame or legal responsibility be held against the publisher, or author, for any damages, reparation, or monetary loss due to the information contained within this book. Either directly or indirectly. You are responsible for your own choices, actions, and results.

Legal Notice:

This book is copyright protected. This book is only for personal use. You cannot amend, distribute, sell, use, quote or paraphrase any part, of the content within this book, without the consent of the author or publisher.

Disclaimer Notice:

Please note the information contained within this document is for educational and entertainment purposes only. All effort has been expended to present accurate, up-to-date, and reliable, complete information. No warranties of any kind are declared or implied. Readers acknowledge that the author is not engaging in the rendering of legal, financial, medical or professional advice. The content within this book has been derived from various sources. Please consult a licensed professional before attempting any techniques outlined in this book.

By reading this document, the reader agrees that under no circumstances is the author responsible for any losses, direct or indirect, which are incurred as a result of the use of the information contained within this document, including, but not limited to, — errors, omissions, or inaccuracies.

Contents

Other Books by Victor Nyx	1
Introduction	2
1. Frankenstein	7
2. The Strange Case of Dr. Jekyll and Mr. Hyde	21
3. The Call of Cthulhu	35
4. The Shining	51
5. Misery	70
Shine a Light on the Power of Dreams	86
References	88

Other Books by Victor Nyx

Dream Interpretation Decoded: Explore Science, Spirituality & Cultural Influences When Understanding Signs and Symbols in Your Dreams

Introduction

Nightmares as the Wellspring of Creativity

Dreams have long been a source of fascination, inspiration, and even dread. They provide a bridge between the subconscious and the conscious, revealing the deepest fears, desires, and mysteries of the human mind.

But what happens when a nightmare—a vision so terrifying it lingers upon waking—transcends the realm of sleep and takes on a life of its own? Some of the most iconic literary works in history were born from the nocturnal terrors of their authors, manifesting into stories that have shaped literature, culture, and our very understanding of horror, identity, and the unknown.

This book explores the profound connection between nightmares and creativity, delving into the stories of four legendary authors who transformed their darkest dreams into literary masterpieces. From Mary Shelley's "Frankenstein" to Stephen King's "Misery", these works owe their origins to moments of fear and revelation that struck their creators in the dead of night. Each chapter is dedicated to one of these authors, breaking down the genesis of their nightmares and how they evolved into some of the most influential stories ever written.

To provide an in-depth exploration of these nightmare-fueled works, each chapter follows a structured analysis, examining ten key aspects of the book and its creation:

1. The Author's Life at the Time of Writing

Before delving into the nightmares themselves, we first look at the personal and professional circumstances of each author when they wrote their novel. Where were they in their careers? What struggles were they facing? Were they in the throes of hardship or triumph? This section paints a picture of their state of mind, giving us clues as to why their subconscious may have conjured such chilling visions.

2. Synopsis of the Storyline

To fully appreciate the impact of each nightmare, we explore the novel's plot in detail. Whether it's Dr. Frankenstein's tragic attempt to create life, the dual nature of Dr. Jekyll and Mr. Hyde, or the creeping cosmic horror of "The Call of Cthulhu", we provide a full summary to set the stage for our analysis.

3. Context of Creation

Every book is a product of its time, reflecting the social, political, and scientific climate in which it was written. This section places the work within its historical context, examining how the era influenced its themes, characters, and settings. Did Shelley's scientific curiosity shape "Frankenstein"? Did Victorian struggles about morality and repression feed into "Dr. Jekyll and Mr. Hyde"? We investigate these intersections between history and fiction.

4. The Dream That Inspired It

This is where the heart of our exploration lies. Each of these authors had a specific nightmare that acted as a catalyst for their story. From Mary Shelley's waking dream of a scientist giving life to a monstrous creation to Stephen King's terrifying vision of his son being chased through the halls of an empty hotel, we examine these moments of inspiration in detail. Using diary entries, interviews, and firsthand accounts, we uncover how each author processed their dream and recognized its narrative potential.

5. Dream Elements That Influenced the Work

Once we establish the dream itself, we break down how its elements found their way into the finished novel. Which characters, settings, or themes were directly lifted from the nightmare? What aspects were altered or expanded upon? In some cases, entire plots emerged from a single haunting image; in others, the dream was merely the spark that set the creative process in motion.

6. Turning the Dream into a Novel

Transforming a fleeting nightmare into a fully realized literary work is no small feat. This section explores the creative process—how each author developed their dream into a novel, what challenges they faced in translating its horror onto the page, and how they expanded upon the initial concept. Was the dream enough to shape the entire story, or did it require further refinement?

7. The Legacy of the Dream

The influence of these nightmares did not end with the publication of their respective novels. Here, we examine how each dream continued to shape the author's career, affecting their future works and personal philosophies. Did Lovecraft's cosmic horrors reappear in his later stories? Did King's nightmares influence more than one of his books? We trace the lasting impact of these visions.

8. Universal Themes of the Dream

One of the most fascinating aspects of nightmares is their universality. Though these authors experienced deeply personal fears, their dreams contained elements that resonate with all of us. In this section, we explore how these nightmares tap into broader human worries—fear of the unknown, loss of control, the fragility of identity—and how readers can relate to them on a deeply personal level.

9. The Power of Dreams in Creativity

Beyond the individual nightmares that shaped these books, we reflect on the broader role of dreams in the creative process. Dreams are an inexhaustible wellspring of inspiration, providing unique perspectives, surreal imagery, and unfiltered emotion. This section discusses how dreams function as a tool for artistic expression, showing how the subconscious mind can be harnessed to generate compelling narratives.

10. Cultural Impact and Significance

Finally, we assess the lasting cultural impact of these works. How were they received at the time of publication? How have they influenced literature, film, and popular culture? From "Frankenstein's" pioneering role in science fiction to "The Shining's" enduring legacy as a masterpiece of horror, we explore how these novels have left an indelible mark on the world.

A Journey into the Nightmares of Great Minds

As you read through this book, you will not only gain insight into the creative minds of Mary Shelley, Robert Louis Stevenson, H.P. Lovecraft, and Stephen King, but you will also be invited to reflect on the role of dreams in your own life. Have you ever awoken from a nightmare so vivid it felt real? Could your own subconscious be hiding the seeds of an incredible story? By examining these authors and their works, we uncover the strange and powerful link between fear, imagination, and storytelling.

The nightmares of these writers changed the course of literary history. Now, we delve into their minds to discover how moments of terror and revelation in the dead of night became some of the most unforgettable tales ever told. Prepare to journey into the dark corridors of dreams—where nightmares do not fade upon waking, but instead take shape in ink and paper, ready to haunt the world forever.

Chapter 1

Frankenstein
by Mary Shelley

"Frankenstein"; or, "The Modern Prometheus" was first published anonymously on January 1, 1818, when Mary Shelley was just 20 years old. It is widely regarded as one of the earliest science fiction novels. Shelley's name did not appear on the book until the second edition, published on August 11, 1823. The novel emerged during a tumultuous period in Mary's life, marked by personal and societal upheaval, including the recent suicide of her half-sister, Fanny Imlay—an event that influenced the novel's themes of despair and loss.

Born to renowned intellectuals—philosopher William Godwin and writer Mary Wollstonecraft—Mary was raised in a world of radical thought and literary influence. However, her mother died shortly after her birth, leaving a void that shaped much of her emotional and creative life.

At the time she conceived "Frankenstein", Mary was in a controversial relationship with poet Percy Bysshe Shelley, who was still married to his first wife, Harriet Westbrook. Their elopement led to financial struggles and social ostracism. Adding to her personal grief, Mary suffered the loss of her first child in 1815, an experience that profoundly affected her and deeply influenced "Frankenstein's" exploration of creation, abandonment, and loss.

Surrounded by literary greatness, Mary found inspiration in the intellectual circles she moved in. She corresponded and socialized with Lord Byron, whose presence at Villa Diodati in the summer of 1816 played a crucial role in "Frankenstein's" genesis. It was Byron who proposed a ghost story challenge to the group, prompting Mary's imagination to conceive the chilling vision that would become her novel. Her writing was also shaped by the works of Romantic poets such as Samuel Taylor Coleridge and John Keats, as well as contemporary scientific theories on galvanism, reanimation, and the nature of life.

The title "Frankenstein" refers to Victor Frankenstein, the novel's protagonist—a young scientist whose ambitious experiment brings a creature to life, only for him to face devastating consequences. The subtitle, "The Modern Prometheus", draws a parallel to the Greek myth of Prometheus, who defied the gods by giving fire to humanity, symbolizing knowledge and creation that come with perilous consequences. Through "Frankenstein", Shelley explores the boundaries of scientific ambition and the moral responsibilities that accompany creation, themes that remain relevant to this day.

Synopsis of the Storyline

"Frankenstein" begins as a series of letters written by Captain Robert Walton to his sister Margaret. While exploring the Arctic, Walton's crew discovers Victor Frankenstein, near death and pursuing something across the frozen wasteland. Victor shares his cautionary tale with Walton.

As a young scientist in Geneva, Victor became consumed by the possibility of creating life itself. Over approximately two years, he studied chemistry and anatomy, gathering materials from dissecting rooms and slaughterhouses to construct his creation. In his laboratory, he succeeded in bringing his creature to life, only to be horrified by the monster's hideous appearance. Victor fled, abandoning his creation.

The creature, despite his frightening visage, possessed intelligence and sensitivity. He learned language by observing a poor family and attempted to make human connections. Yet society universally rejected him due to his appearance. This rejection transformed the creature's loneliness into rage and a desire for revenge against his creator.

The creature systematically destroyed Victor's life, murdering his younger brother William. To further torment Victor, the creature placed a locket belonging to William into the pocket of Justine Moritz, the family's servant, leading to her wrongful conviction and execution.

Later, after Victor destroyed the unfinished female companion, the creature killed Victor's best friend, Henry Clerval. Finally, when Victor refused to create a female companion for him, the creature murdered Victor's bride, Elizabeth, on their wedding night.

Consumed by grief and vengeance, Victor pursued the creature into the Arctic. There, he encountered Walton's expedition before succumbing to exhaustion and exposure. The creature appeared on Walton's ship to mourn over Victor's body, expressing remorse while maintaining that Victor's cruel abandonment led to his acts of violence. The creature then disappeared into the Arctic wilderness, intending to end his own existence.

Context of Creation

In the summer of 1816, dark clouds loomed over Lake Geneva, Switzerland, where a group of literary minds gathered at the Villa Diodati. The eruption of Mount Tambora in 1815 had released vast amounts of volcanic ash into the atmosphere, leading to significant climate anomalies in 1816, a period often referred to as the "Year Without a Summer." This resulted in unusually cold and dreary weather, with persistent "dry fog" and reduced sunlight, creating an eerie and oppressive atmosphere.

Mary Godwin (soon to be Mary Shelley) found herself in distinguished company: her future husband Percy Bysshe Shelley, the notorious poet Lord Byron, Byron's physician John Polidori, and Mary's stepsister Claire Clairmont. Confined indoors by the relentless rain, the group passed their evenings reading German ghost stories from "Fantasmagoriana" and discussing the latest scientific theories.

One night, Byron proposed a challenge - each person should write their own supernatural tale. While the others quickly began their stories, Mary struggled to find inspiration. She listened intently to conversations between Percy and Byron about galvanism - the theory that electricity could reanimate dead tissue - and the experiments of Erasmus Darwin, who claimed to have made dead matter move.

The breakthrough came during a sleepless night. In her own words, Mary "saw with shut eyes... the hideous phantasm of a man stretched out, and then, on the working of some powerful engine, show signs of life." This vivid waking dream, born from the intersection of Gothic horror and cutting-edge science, became the seed of "Frankenstein".

At just eighteen years old, Mary began expanding her ghost story into a novel. Her tale reflected deeper concerns of the Romantic era: humanity's relationship with nature, the dangers of unchecked ambition, and the moral responsibilities of creators toward their creations. The scientific advances of the Industrial Revolution provided a backdrop for her exploration of what happens when human ingenuity overreaches its bounds.

The novel was published anonymously in 1818, with a preface written by Percy Shelley, leading many to initially believe he was the author. It wasn't until the second edition in 1823 that Mary Shelley was credited as the creator of this enduring masterpiece.

The Dream That Inspired It

Mary Shelley famously described the nightmare that inspired "Frankenstein" in her 1831 introduction to the novel. She recounted that during a night of storytelling with Percy Shelley, Lord Byron, and others in the summer of 1816, she struggled to think of a story as compelling as those of her companions. After several days of creative frustration, she experienced a vivid dream:

"I saw the pale student of unhallowed arts kneeling beside the thing he had put together. I saw the hideous phantasm of a man stretched out, and then, on the working of some powerful engine, show signs of life, and stir with an uneasy, half-vital motion."

In this nightmare, Mary envisioned Victor Frankenstein infusing life into his creation—a horrifying yet poignant image of life created unnaturally. The scene captured the terrifying potential of human ambition and scientific experimentation.

Reflecting on this experience, Shelley wrote:

"When I placed my head upon my pillow, I did not sleep, nor could I be said to think... I saw with shut eyes, but acute mental vision."

This state between sleeping and waking, known as hypnagogia, allowed her to experience the scene with remarkable detail.

Her dream answered a question posed by Lord Byron and her husband, Percy Shelley: 'what if a man could create life'? The dream struck her as a natural seed for a story that would explore the boundaries of human ambition and the moral responsibilities of creation.

Dream Elements that Influenced the Work

Mary Shelley's nightmare gave rise to more than just a story—it solidified deep fears about scientific progress and human nature that defined her time. The "pale student" she saw in her dream became Victor Frankenstein, a man whose brilliance turned to madness through isolation and unchecked ambition. His character reflected the Romantic era's anxieties about where uncontrolled scientific discovery might lead.

In her dream, the creature's first moments of life—described as an "uneasy, half-vital motion"—captured the terror of tampering with nature. This chilling image became the novel's pivotal scene, where Victor's creation opens its "dull yellow eyes" for the first time. That moment symbolized both a great achievement and a terrible mistake, marking the line between triumph and transgression.

Shelley's nightmare didn't just shape the plot—it defined the novel's deeper philosophical themes. The boundary between life and death became blurred, raising questions about the soul, consciousness, and what truly makes us human. Victor's "unhallowed arts" challenged divine authority, while the creature's suffering forced readers to confront themes of responsibility and abandonment.

The novel's Gothic atmosphere was also born from Shelley's nightmare. The eerie laboratory, crackling electricity, and the creature's horrifying appearance all stemmed from that single haunting vision. Yet beneath these classic horror elements lay deeper ideas about parental duty and the consequences of rejecting one's own creation.

The creature's violent "birth," unlike natural reproduction, reflected society's unease with scientific advancements and materialism. Victor's laboratory became a distorted version of childbirth, where electricity and chemistry replaced nature. This unsettling contrast reinforced the novel's warning about human arrogance in the face of nature's mysteries.

Turning the Dream into A Novel

Mary Shelley's nightmare sparked the idea for *Frankenstein*, but it was far from a fully formed story. Turning her chilling vision of a "pale student of unhallowed arts" bringing life to a grotesque creature into a complete novel was a daunting challenge. While the dream provided a powerful foundation, Shelley had to develop its fragmented imagery into a structured narrative.

She didn't just explore the act of creation—she also examined its ethical, emotional, and social consequences. In her introduction to the novel, she reflected on the difficulty of shaping her chaotic vision into a coherent work, writing:

"Invention, it must be humbly admitted, does not consist in creating out of void, but out of chaos."

To build her story, Shelley incorporated contemporary scientific debates, particularly galvanism and the possibility of reanimating dead tissue—ideas that fascinated early 19th-century thinkers. These scientific influences gave "Frankenstein" a sense of realism, while also grounding it in the broader intellectual currents of the time. She blended Enlightenment ideals, which emphasized reason and discovery, with Romantic concerns about the dangers of unchecked progress.

Shelley's personal life also deeply shaped the novel. She had recently lost an infant daughter, an experience that left her grappling with themes of life, death, and creation. Her complex relationship with her father, philosopher William Godwin, infused *Frankenstein* with themes of parental responsibility and abandonment. These personal struggles shaped the dynamic between Victor and his creature, making it far more than a simple horror story.

Her grief, along with her intellectual exchanges with Percy Shelley and Lord Byron, influenced her exploration of mortality, isolation, and the destructive potential of unrestrained ambition. These deeply personal experiences gave the novel a raw emotional intensity, making its themes resonate with readers across generations.

To expand on her dream's imagery, Shelley created complex characters that embodied its central themes. Victor Frankenstein became a tragic figure, representing the dangers of arrogance and the moral blindness that can come with unchecked ambition.

Meanwhile, the creature—originally a voiceless "phantasm" in her nightmare—evolved into an intelligent, emotionally rich being whose longing for acceptance made his story both poignant and tragic. Through this transformation, Shelley explored the consequences of alienation and the universal human need for connection, giving her novel timeless relevance.

Another challenge was maintaining the eerie tone of her nightmare throughout the novel. She achieved this by using Gothic settings such as the desolate Arctic, the stormy Alps, and Victor's dark laboratory. These environments mirrored the characters' psychological turmoil and heightened the novel's haunting, dreamlike quality.

Ultimately, Mary Shelley's ability to turn a single nightmare into "Frankenstein" was a testament to her unique blend of personal experience, intellectual depth, and creative vision. The dream may have planted the seed, but it was her ability to expand on it—infusing it with science, philosophy, and emotion—that made it a masterpiece. Her work remains a powerful example of how imagination can transform raw, chaotic visions into enduring art.

Legacy of the Dream

Mary Shelley's dream that inspired "Frankenstein" has left an enduring legacy, shaping not only the literary world but also broader cultural discussions about science, morality, and creation. The novel, often regarded as the first work of science fiction, set the foundation for a genre that explores the ethical and social implications of scientific progress.

Its themes—human ambition, the limits of science, the responsibilities of creators, and the dangers of tampering with nature—remain relevant today. The novel continues to influence debates about artificial intelligence, genetic engineering, and other technological advancements. Shelley's "waking vision" of unnatural life became a powerful symbol of imagination's ability to explore human fears and possibilities, inspiring countless works in literature and film.

"Frankenstein" became the defining work of Shelley's career, elevating her literary reputation but also overshadowing her subsequent works. Though she wrote other notable novels like "The Last Man" and "Valperga", none achieved the fame or cultural impact of "Frankenstein".

The themes of loss, isolation, and ambition—shaped by her personal experiences of grief and alienation—continued to appear in her later writing. The deaths of her children and her husband, Percy Shelley, deeply affected her, and her works often reflect profound questions about mortality and the human condition.

While "Frankenstein" brought her literary fame, it also confined her identity to that singular masterpiece, despite her ongoing efforts to showcase her versatility through novels, short stories, and essays.

The legacy of Mary Shelley's dream extends far beyond her own career. Her ability to blend science, philosophy, and deep emotion in "Frankenstein" established a precedent for speculative fiction and inspired countless writers, from H.G. Wells to Margaret Atwood.

Her exploration of scientific overreach and her nuanced portrayal of the "monster" archetype resonated with Romantic-era concerns and continues to captivate modern audiences. Ultimately, her dream symbolizes the power of imagination to turn a fleeting vision into an enduring work of art.

Through "Frankenstein", Shelley not only defined her own career but also left an indelible mark on the literary world. Shelley's ability to channel her nightmare into a powerful literary work has ensured that "Frankenstein" continues to challenge, inspire, and provoke readers and thinkers to this day.

Universal Themes of the Dream

The universal themes in dreams that lead to creative works often tap into our deepest fears, desires, and questions about mortality. Mary Shelley's nightmare that inspired "Frankenstein" resonates with fundamental human uncertainties that persist across cultures and time periods. The image of a scientist bringing life to lifeless matter speaks to humanity's eternal struggle with death and our desire to overcome our mortal limitations.

Readers can connect with the primal fear of playing God and disturbing the natural order - a theme that surfaces in many people's own dreams of loss of control or unintended consequences. The cold, dead eyes suddenly opening that Shelley described mirrors common dream imagery of the lifeless becoming animated, reflecting our subconscious wrestling with questions of what truly separates life from death.

The theme of creation and responsibility that emerged from Shelley's dream touches on universal parental concerns. Many readers may recognize their own dreams of failing their children or creating something they cannot control. The monster's abandonment by his creator taps into deep-seated fears of rejection and isolation that frequently manifest in dreams.

Shelley's dream also captured the timeless human desire to push boundaries and achieve the impossible, even at great cost. Readers can relate this to their own ambitious dreams, both literal and metaphorical, where the line between innovation and hubris becomes blurred. The visceral horror of her nightmare connects to our collective unease about scientific advancement outpacing moral consideration - a concern that remains remarkably relevant two centuries later.

The dream's themes of life, death, and the consequences of human ambition provide readers a lens through which to examine their own relationship with mortality and ethical boundaries. By exploring how Shelley's subconscious fears manifested in her dream and subsequent novel, readers can better understand how their own dreams might reflect deeper truths about themselves and their place in the world.

Power of Dreams in Creativity

The raw creative power of dreams has fascinated artists and writers throughout history. In Mary Shelley's case, her nightmare became the catalyst for one of literature's most enduring stories. During that fateful summer evening in 1816, as rain pattered against the windows of Villa Diodati, Shelley's unconscious mind unleashed imagery that would reshape gothic literature forever.

Dreams operate outside the constraints of logic and reason. In that twilight space between sleeping and waking, Shelley's mind freely combined her fears about childbirth, her interest in galvanism, and the scientific discussions she'd witnessed between her husband Percy and Lord Byron.

The nightmare's potency stemmed from its ability to bypass Shelley's conscious mind and tap directly into her deepest sufferings. At just eighteen years old, she had already experienced the joy and terror of creation through childbirth, and the devastating loss of her first baby. These raw emotions emerged in her dream as the student's horror at his own creation - a scene that would become central to her novel.

The nightmare provided Shelley with more than just dramatic imagery. The surreal logic of her nightmare - where death transforms into life through scientific means - gave her the framework to explore profound questions about human nature and responsibility. The dream's emotional impact drove her to expand a simple ghost story into a complex meditation on ambition, creation, and abandonment.

Many artists have discovered that dreams offer a unique creative laboratory where ideas can merge and mutate freely. In Shelley's case, her nightmare didn't just provide the initial spark - it offered a sustained source of imagery and emotional truth that she could draw upon throughout the writing process. The dream's influence can be felt in the novel's atmospheric descriptions, its exploration of the boundary between life and death, and its deep psychological insights into both creator and creation.

Cultural Impact and Significance

The cultural footprint of "Frankenstein" reaches far beyond its origins as a Gothic novel. The story penetrated deep into society's consciousness, spawning countless adaptations that transformed Shelley's creation into a universal symbol of scientific hubris and moral responsibility.

In cinema, the 1931 film adaptation starring Boris Karloff cemented the creature's iconic image - the flat-topped head, neck bolts, and greenish skin became instantly recognizable elements of pop culture. This visualization, though far removed from Shelley's description, created an enduring archetype that persists in everything from Halloween costumes to breakfast cereals.

The term "Frankenstein" entered common language as shorthand for dangerous scientific advancement without ethical consideration. From GMOs dubbed "Frankenfood" to debates about cloning and artificial intelligence, Shelley's cautionary tale provides a framework for discussing the boundaries of human innovation.

In academia, the novel sparked new literary genres and critical discussions. As one of the earliest examples of science fiction, it helped establish the genre's tradition of using scientific advancement as a lens to examine human nature. The work's exploration of creation, responsibility, and the consequences of abandonment continues to fuel philosophical and ethical debates in fields ranging from bioethics to artificial intelligence.

Medical science particularly feels Shelley's influence. As researchers push boundaries with genetic engineering, synthetic biology, and artificial organ development, the ethical questions raised in "Frankenstein" remain startlingly relevant. The novel serves as a touchstone for discussions about scientific responsibility and the moral implications of creating or modifying life.

The story's influence extends into modern literature and media, with countless retellings and reimagining. From serious dramatic adaptations to playful parodies like "Young Frankenstein," the basic elements of Shelley's narrative prove infinitely adaptable while maintaining their power to provoke thought and discussion about humanity's relationship with scientific progress.

Chapter 2

The Strange Case of Dr. Jekyll and Mr. Hyde
by Robert Louis Stevenson

At the time Robert Louis Stevenson dreamed of and wrote "The Strange Case of Dr. Jekyll and Mr. Hyde", his life was defined by both profound creativity and significant personal challenges. Published in January 1886, the novella marked a turning point in Stevenson's career as a writer.

By 1886, Stevenson had already achieved literary success with works like "Treasure Island" (1883) and "A Child's Garden of Verses" (1885). However, "Dr. Jekyll and Mr. Hyde" significantly enhanced his reputation and is often considered one of his most enduring works.

He was 35 years old and already married to Fanny Osbourne, an American divorcee who had been a crucial source of support in his life. Fanny played an active role in his work, providing editorial advice and encouragement as he developed his ideas.

Despite his growing literary success, Stevenson's health was precarious. He suffered from chronic respiratory illnesses, likely tuberculosis, which frequently left him bedridden. This physical frailty shaped much of his daily life and forced him to write under difficult circumstances.

During this time, Stevenson lived with his wife in Bournemouth, a seaside town in southern England. They resided in a home named "Skerryvore," which Stevenson named after a Scottish lighthouse built by his uncle, Alan Stevenson. The home was chosen for its coastal location, which was thought to have therapeutic benefits for his chronic respiratory health issues.

Despite his illness, Stevenson maintained an active intellectual life and corresponded with other prominent writers of the era, including Henry James, who greatly admired his work. These exchanges were important for Stevenson, offering inspiration and camaraderie during a time of physical isolation.

The title of the novel was partly inspired by Stevenson's fascination with Scottish history and geography. The surname "Hyde" is thought to be a play on the word "hide," reflecting the hidden, darker aspects of the character, while "Jekyll" was borrowed from Reverend Walter Jekyll, a former Anglican clergyman and friend of Stevenson. The novel explores themes of morality, identity, and the darker sides of human nature, themes that resonated deeply with Victorian readers.

At the time of its publication, Stevenson faced not only personal health struggles but also financial pressures. He hoped that "Dr. Jekyll and Mr. Hyde" would achieve commercial success, and it did, becoming an immediate bestseller. Within the first six months of its release, the novel sold close to 40,000 copies in Britain.

Despite the challenges he faced, Stevenson's ability to transform his adversities into timeless literature remains a testament to his resilience and creativity. "Dr. Jekyll and Mr. Hyde" continues to be celebrated as a masterpiece that delves into the complexities of the human psyche, reflecting both Stevenson's personal struggles and his literary genius. The novel explores themes of duality and the interplay of good and evil within individuals, concepts that have resonated deeply with readers since its publication.

Synopsis of the Storyline

In Victorian London's fog-laden streets, the story unfolds through the eyes of Gabriel John Utterson, a reserved lawyer whose concern for his friend Dr. Henry Jekyll leads him down a path of disturbing revelations. Utterson becomes concerned when he learns that Jekyll has made a sinister man named Edward Hyde the beneficiary of his will, bequeathing his wealth to Hyde in the event of his death or disappearance.

Utterson finds Hyde to be cruel and repulsive and becomes determined to uncover the connection between the two men. He learns that Hyde has been involved in a number of violent and disturbing incidents, including the brutal trampling of a young girl. Despite this, Dr. Jekyll continues to associate with Hyde, and Utterson becomes more alarmed as Jekyll's behavior grows increasingly erratic.

As Utterson investigates further, he discovers that Jekyll and Hyde share a mysterious and unsettling connection. Eventually, Utterson is invited to Jekyll's house, where he finds the doctor in a distressed state. Jekyll assures him that he is working to rid himself of Hyde, but the situation worsens, and Jekyll isolates himself from the outside world. The mystery deepens when, after a period of disappearance, Hyde vanishes entirely. Utterson is left with many unanswered questions, and the tension builds until the final revelation.

The truth comes to light when Jekyll's butler, Poole, seeks Utterson's help, fearing for his master's safety. They break into Jekyll's laboratory and discover Hyde's lifeless body dressed in Jekyll's clothes. Later, through Jekyll's written confession, Utterson learns that Dr. Jekyll and Edward Hyde are the same person.

Jekyll had created a potion that allowed him to transform into Hyde, enabling him to act out his darker impulses without tarnishing his respectable public image. However, over time, Jekyll loses control of the transformation, and Hyde's evil nature begins to dominate. In the end, Jekyll is consumed by Hyde, leading to his tragic demise.

Context of Creation

In the bustling world of Victorian London, Robert Louis Stevenson found himself at a crossroads. The year was 1885, and he resided in Bournemouth, a seaside town where he sought relief from his chronic respiratory ailments. His family's financial situation remained precarious despite his growing literary reputation, and the pressure to produce successful work weighed heavily on him.

The Victorian era's rigid social structure and moral codes permeated every aspect of life. Cities expanded rapidly as industrialization transformed the landscape, creating stark contrasts between wealth and poverty, respectability and vice. Scientific discoveries challenged traditional religious beliefs, while new psychological theories suggested darker aspects of human nature lurking beneath civilized facades.

Stevenson's own experiences in Edinburgh's medical community had exposed him to the period's fascination with the relationship between mind and body. He witnessed how respected doctors and lawyers led double lives, maintaining spotless reputations while secretly indulging in gambling dens and opium houses.

Stevenson was also familiar with the tale of Deacon Brodie, an 18th-century Edinburgh cabinetmaker and city councilor who led a double life as a burglar. This duality of Victorian society - the contrast between public virtue and private vice - became a central element of his work.

During this time, Stevenson suffered from frequent fever-induced nightmares. His illness confined him to bed for long periods, where he relied on his imagination and memories of Edinburgh's dark wynds and closes - the narrow alleyways where respectability disappeared after nightfall. These atmospheric elements would later infuse his portrayal of London in the novel.

The period's preoccupation with scientific advancement also influenced the work's creation. Darwin's theories had shaken religious certainties, while new discoveries in chemistry and medicine raised questions about the boundaries of scientific ethics. Stevenson incorporated these contemporary doubts into his tale, using Jekyll's experiments to explore the potential dangers of unchecked scientific progress.

The Dream that Inspired It

On a cold autumn night in 1885, while battling a severe fever in Bournemouth, Robert Louis Stevenson experienced the nightmare that would birth his most famous work. Bedridden and delirious, Stevenson plunged into a dream so vivid and terrifying that his wife Fanny was forced to wake him as he thrashed and moaned in his sleep.

In his "A Chapter on Dreams," published in Scribner's Magazine, Stevenson detailed how his "Brownies" - his term for the subconscious creative forces that worked while he slept - presented him with the core elements of Jekyll and Hyde. The nightmare revealed a man who could transform himself through scientific means, along with two specific scenes that would become pivotal to the novel.

The first scene showed a figure mixing chemicals to create a transformative potion. The second, which Stevenson described as "the scene at the window," depicted a figure witnessing a transformation. These dream sequences so gripped Stevenson that upon being awakened, he immediately began outlining the story despite his illness.

Stevenson also emphasized how the dream's intensity surpassed ordinary nightmares. The visceral horror of watching a man's identity split and transform resonated with themes that had long preoccupied him - the duality of human nature and the thin veneer between civilization and savagery.

When Fanny expressed concern about his agitated state during the dream, Stevenson reportedly responded with excitement rather than fear, recognizing the creative potential in his nightmare. The dream's imagery aligned perfectly with his desire to explore Victorian society's hypocrisies and the psychological complexity of human nature. This incident underscores how Stevenson's subconscious mind provided the vivid scenes that became central to his exploration of the duality inherent in human nature.

Within three days of the dream, Stevenson had completed the first draft of his "fine bogey tale," though the initial draft met an unexpected fate when Stevenson's wife, Fanny, criticized it for being overly allegorical. In response, Stevenson burned the manuscript and rewrote the story entirely, focusing on crafting a gripping horror tale while retaining the deeper themes of morality and identity. The rewritten version struck a perfect balance, captivating readers with its chilling narrative and thought-provoking insights.

Dream Elements that Influenced the Work

The nightmare's visceral imagery played a pivotal role in shaping "The Strange Case of Dr. Jekyll and Mr. Hyde", influencing its characters, scenes, and themes. The central concept of duality and transformation came directly from the nightmare, in which Stevenson saw a man undergoing a split in identity, turning from one persona into another. This inspired the novel's exploration of the conflict between good and evil within an individual.

The dream also included imagery of a man mixing chemicals and consuming a potion, resulting in a horrifying transformation. These visuals directly influenced the laboratory scenes, where Dr. Jekyll creates and uses his mysterious potion to become Mr. Hyde.

Additionally, Stevenson's dream contained the "scene at the window," where a figure undergoes a visible transformation, shocking an onlooker. This moment became one of the novel's most dramatic and eerie sequences, adding to the psychological horror of the story.

The visceral sensations Stevenson experienced in the dream, such as grinding bones and the feeling of an identity being stripped away, also contributed to the vivid descriptions of Jekyll's transformations.

The grotesque figure in the dream, unrestrained by morality or societal expectations, inspired the creation of Edward Hyde, a character who embodies Jekyll's suppressed evil nature. Hyde's small, deformed stature symbolizes the moral corruption he represents.

The unsettling and surreal atmosphere of Stevenson's dream is reflected in the novel's setting, with its foggy, shadowy London streets and claustrophobic environments that mirror the oppressive, nightmarish tone of the dreamscape.

Finally, the fragmented nature of Stevenson's dream, with shocking revelations unfolding piece by piece, influenced the novel's non-linear narrative structure. The truth about Jekyll and Hyde is revealed gradually through letters, testimonies, and dramatic events, heightening suspense and horror.

Stevenson later described the dream as a creative gift, noting how his subconscious, or "Brownies," provided him with a fully formed concept that he immediately began to develop into a story. These elements combined to create one of the most enduring works of Gothic fiction, deeply rooted in Stevenson's feverish vision.

Turning the Dream into A Novel

While the dream provided Stevenson with the core concept and key scenes, transforming this raw material into a polished narrative proved challenging. The initial draft, completed in three feverish days, faced criticism from Stevenson's wife, Fanny, who found it overly allegorical, leading to its destruction.

Fanny Stevenson's critical feedback proved crucial as she recognized that the first version didn't fully explore the deeper implications of the dream's imagery. After burning this draft, Stevenson approached the rewrite with a broader vision, expanding beyond the simple transformation story to examine Victorian society's hypocrisies and the internal struggles of human nature.

In the second version, Stevenson crafted a sophisticated narrative structure. Rather than directly presenting Jekyll and Hyde's duality, he built suspense through multiple viewpoints, allowing readers to gradually uncover the truth. The dream's vivid scenes of transformation became anchor points around which he wove a larger mystery.

The author enhanced the dream's basic premise by incorporating contemporary concerns about scientific advancement and social propriety. Jekyll's experiments reflected Victorian concerns about unchecked scientific progress, while Hyde embodied fears about degradation and atavism. Stevenson drew from his legal training to add credible details about wills and contracts, grounding the fantastic elements in realistic procedures.

Stevenson also expanded the philosophical implications beyond what the dream suggested. Through Jekyll's detailed confession in the final chapter, he explored questions of free will, addiction, and the nature of consciousness. The author's own experiences with illness and mortality informed his portrayal of Jekyll's desperate attempts to transcend human limitations.

The resulting novel transformed a nightmare's raw horror into a sophisticated exploration of human duality. Stevenson maintained the dream's visceral impact while adding layers of social commentary and psychological insight that resonated with Victorian readers and continue to engage modern audiences.

Legacy of the Dream

The phenomenal success of Jekyll and Hyde transformed Stevenson's career trajectory. While he had achieved recognition with earlier works like "Treasure Island", the dream-inspired novel elevated him to literary stardom. The story's psychological depth marked a shift from his adventure tales to more complex explorations of human nature.

In his subsequent works, Stevenson continued mining the rich territory first revealed in his fever dream. "The Master of Ballantrae" delved deeper into the concept of dueling identities, while later short stories like "Markheim" explored moral ambiguity and internal conflict. The dream had unlocked a darker, more introspective vein in his writing that complemented his natural storytelling abilities.

The novel's impact extended far beyond Stevenson's lifetime. Its exploration of split personalities influenced early psychological research, with Carl Jung referencing the work in his studies of the shadow self. The term "Jekyll and Hyde" entered common language as shorthand for dual nature, showing how deeply the dream-born story resonated with human understanding of identity.

The dream's influence on gothic literature proved equally significant. Stevenson's masterful blend of psychological horror with scientific elements helped establish a new direction for the genre. Writers who followed drew inspiration from his technique of using realistic details to ground supernatural elements, creating more sophisticated horror narratives.

The story's adaptability to different media demonstrated the universal appeal of the dream's core imagery. From early stage productions to countless film versions, the visceral transformation scenes first glimpsed in Stevenson's nightmare retained their power to captivate audiences. Each new adaptation found fresh relevance in the dream's themes of identity and moral struggle.

Through Jekyll and Hyde, Stevenson showed how a single dream could spawn a cultural touchstone that transcended its Victorian origins. The novel's enduring influence proved that dreams could serve as more than mere inspiration - they could tap into fundamental truths about human nature that resonated across generations.

Universal Themes of the Dream

Stevenson's nightmare of transformation struck a deep chord because it embodied universal fears and desires that haunt the human psyche. The image of a respected professional morphing into a violent creature mirrors common troubling dreams where people find themselves suddenly changed or revealed in public. Like Jekyll's transformation, these dreams often reflect fears of losing control or having one's private self exposed.

The dream's theme of duality resonates with the common experience of maintaining different personas - the professional face shown at work versus private behavior at home, or the contrast between social expectations and personal desires. Readers recognize their own internal conflicts in Jekyll's struggle, having experienced moments when their actions didn't align with their self-image.

The nocturnal setting of Hyde's activities connects with universal dream imagery of darkness concealing forbidden acts. Many people experience dreams where nighttime becomes a stage for breaking social rules or expressing repressed impulses. The fog-shrouded London streets in the story echo the murky dreamscapes where people confront their own shadow selves.

Jekyll's addiction to transformation reflects common dreams about losing control to compulsive behaviors. Readers who have struggled with temptation or destructive habits recognize the spiral of rationalization and regret depicted in Jekyll's confession. The story validates these internal battles while warning about their potential consequences.

The dream's central transformation scene taps into primal fears of bodily distortion that frequently appear in nightmares. People often dream of physical changes that represent emotional or psychological states - a universal language of metaphor that Stevenson's story employs masterfully. The visceral horror of Jekyll becoming Hyde speaks to deep-seated angst about identity and self-control.

Through these archetypal elements, Stevenson's dream-inspired narrative provides readers with a framework for examining their own internal conflicts. The story prompts reflection on questions that trouble everyone: How well do we really know ourselves? What parts of our nature do we choose to suppress? What are the costs of denying aspects of who we are?

Power of Dreams in Creativity

Stevenson's nightmare transformation of Jekyll into Hyde demonstrates how dreams can crystallize complex psychological concepts into powerful narrative images. The raw emotional impact of his dream - the horror of witnessing a complete personality change - provided the seed for a story that would resonate across generations. Where conscious writing might have resulted in a more cerebral exploration of duality, the dream-inspired imagery captured the visceral terror of losing control over one's identity.

The dream's influence extends beyond the central transformation scene. The nightmarish atmosphere of fog-bound London streets and the creeping dread of Hyde's midnight wanderings retain the surreal logic of dreams, where meaning emerges through symbol and suggestion rather than explicit statement. This dream-like quality allows the story to operate on multiple levels simultaneously, functioning as both thriller and psychological allegory.

Dreams bypass conscious censorship to reveal deeper truths, and Stevenson's nightmare exposed Victorian concerns about reputation, morality, and the darker impulses that respectable society preferred to ignore. By building on his dream's imagery, he created a work that challenged readers to confront their own hidden selves.

The success of Jekyll and Hyde illustrates how dreams can serve as bridges between personal and universal experience. What began as Stevenson's private nightmare became a shared cultural touchstone precisely because it expressed common fears and desires in the compelling language of dreams. His ability to translate dream imagery into coherent narrative while preserving its primal power shows how creative work can transform individual visions into universal art.

Dreams continue to offer writers and artists direct access to the subconscious mind's unlimited creativity. Like Stevenson, modern creators who pay attention to their dreams may find them containing the seeds of stories that speak to fundamental human experiences and concerns.

Cultural Impact and Significance

When Stevenson's novel hit Victorian bookstores in 1886, it captured the public imagination with unprecedented force. The novel became an immediate sensation, selling 40,000 copies in its first six months and cementing Stevenson's reputation as a master of psychological horror.

Within months, theatrical adaptations appeared on London stages, with actors competing to portray the dramatic transformation between Jekyll and Hyde. The story's examination of duality resonated deeply with Victorian society, where maintaining respectability while grappling with forbidden desires struck a powerful chord.

The work's timing coincided with growing public interest in psychology and criminal behavior. Jack the Ripper's crimes in 1888 only heightened the story's impact, as Londoners saw parallels between the fictional

Hyde and real-world monsters hiding behind respectable facades. The novel influenced emerging detective fiction, particularly in its emphasis on psychological motivation rather than mere puzzle-solving.

In scientific circles, the book sparked debates about human consciousness and personality. Medical journals referenced Jekyll's transformation in discussions of multiple personality disorders, while moral philosophers cited the work when examining questions of free will and responsibility. The story's blend of Gothic horror with scientific speculation helped establish key conventions of the emerging science fiction genre.

The novel's influence extended into other literary works of the period. Oscar Wilde's "The Picture of Dorian Gray" (1890) explored similar themes of hidden corruption, while authors like H.G. Wells incorporated elements of scientific transformation in their works. The "mad scientist" character type, though not entirely original to Stevenson, gained new prominence through Jekyll's cautionary tale.

Beyond entertainment, the story served as a lens through which Victorian society examined its own contradictions. The respectability of Jekyll contrasted with Hyde's brutality reflected widespread concerns about urban crime and social degeneration. The work's enduring popularity demonstrated how effectively it captured the concerns of an era struggling to reconcile rapid scientific advancement with traditional moral values.

Chapter 3

The Call of Cthulhu

by H.P. Lovecraft

In February 1928, H.P. Lovecraft's seminal short story, "The Call of Cthulhu," was published in the pulp magazine "Weird Tales". At that time, Lovecraft was 37 years old, having been born on August 20, 1890, in Providence, Rhode Island.

By 1928, Lovecraft had returned to his hometown of Providence after a tumultuous period in New York City. In 1924, he married Sonia Greene and moved to Brooklyn. However, the marriage faced challenges, including financial difficulties and Lovecraft's discomfort with the city's diverse environment. These factors led to their separation, and Lovecraft's subsequent return to Providence in 1926.

Back in Providence, Lovecraft resided with his aunts, Lillian Delora Phillips and Annie Emeline Phillips, in the family home. His mother had passed away in 1921, and his father had died earlier in 1898 after being institutionalized. These personal losses deeply affected Lovecraft, contributing to his themes of cosmic horror and existential dread.

Financially, Lovecraft struggled throughout his life. He earned a modest income through ghostwriting and revising works for other writers.

Despite his prolific writing, he saw little financial success from his publications. This economic hardship was a constant source of stress and influenced the bleakness present in his works.

Lovecraft maintained extensive correspondence with several contemporary writers, forming what is now known as the "Lovecraft Circle." Notable correspondents included Robert E. Howard, the creator of Conan the Barbarian; Clark Ashton Smith, a poet and author of fantastical fiction; and Frank Belknap Long, a close friend and fellow writer. Through these letters, they shared ideas, critiqued each other's works, and expanded upon shared mythologies.

The name "Cthulhu" is one of Lovecraft's linguistic inventions, designed to be alien and challenging for human pronunciation. In his letters, Lovecraft suggested that the closest approximation in human speech would be "Khlûl'-hloo," emphasizing its inhuman origins. The character Cthulhu itself is described as a colossal entity with an octopus-like head, a scaly, rubbery body, prodigious claws, and narrow wings, embodying the incomprehensible nature of the cosmos that Lovecraft often portrayed.

Synopsis of the Storyline

The story unfolds through a series of documents and accounts discovered by the main character, Francis Wayland Thurston, who investigates the notes of his deceased great-uncle, Professor Angell. Angell's notes detail the strange cult of Cthulhu, a secretive group that worships a massive, ancient being said to slumber in the submerged city of R'lyeh.

This entity, Cthulhu, is described as a monstrous combination of human, octopus, and dragon-like features, radiating an aura of incomprehensible power and malevolence. Thurston's investigation unfolds through several accounts.

The first, *The Horror in Clay*, describes the discovery of a bizarre and unsettling sculpture by artist Henry Anthony Wilcox, who is plagued by nightmarish visions of the monstrous being. Wilcox's dreams are later linked to a wider phenomenon, where people across the world experience similar visions. These shared nightmares point to a deeper, global connection to Cthulhu and its ancient cult.

The second part, *The Tale of Inspector Legrasse*, recounts a police investigation into a strange cult performing ritualistic ceremonies in the swamps of Louisiana. The investigation reveals that these rituals are connected to the worship of Cthulhu, suggesting that this cult has existed for centuries, preserving the knowledge of the entity's power and existence.

The final section, *The Madness from the Sea*, shifts to the account of a Norwegian sailor. Gustaf Johansen recounts how his crew discovered the risen city of R'lyeh during their voyage. Exploring the alien architecture, they inadvertently release Cthulhu from his tomb. The sight of the monstrous entity drives the crew to madness or death. Johansen narrowly escapes by ramming their ship into Cthulhu, causing the creature to temporarily disperse, and survives to tell the tale.

Through these accounts, Thurston pieces together the horrifying reality of Cthulhu—a being of incomprehensible power that has been imprisoned beneath the sea for eons. The cult believes that one day, Cthulhu will awaken, rise from the depths, and reclaim the Earth, bringing ruin to humanity.

Thurston realizes the terrifying truth: humanity is insignificant in the face of such ancient cosmic forces, and the knowledge of Cthulhu's existence is enough to drive the human mind to madness. The story ends with a sense of foreboding, as Thurston acknowledges the inevitable return of Cthulhu and the helplessness of humankind against such a vast, unknowable power.

Context of Creation

H.P. Lovecraft conceived the idea for "The Call of Cthulhu" during the mid-1920s, a period marked by significant personal and societal challenges. At the time, Lovecraft was grappling with financial instability and living in relative seclusion in Providence, Rhode Island. He wrote the story in the summer of 1926, reflecting his experiences and the broader societal apprehensions of the era.

His brief marriage to Sonia Greene had ended in separation, and his reluctance to embrace urban life in New York City led him back to his hometown, where he retreated into his world of writing and correspondence. Lovecraft relied heavily on his pen-pal network of fellow writers and enthusiasts, which served as both a creative outlet and a source of intellectual camaraderie.

The work was written during the 1920s, a decade characterized by rapid modernization, the aftermath of World War I, and a growing interest in science, psychology, and the occult. These elements are deeply reflected in "The Call of Cthulhu".

The story's themes of ancient, unknowable forces juxtaposed with modern scientific inquiry mirror the tensions of the time, as humanity grappled with the implications of new discoveries and the fragility of civilization. Lovecraft's exploration of cosmic insignificance aligns with post-war disillusionment and a growing awareness of humanity's vulnerability in the face of greater, uncontrollable forces.

The specific inspiration for "The Call of Cthulhu" is believed to have come from a combination of Lovecraft's dreams and his intellectual interests. He was deeply influenced by his own nightmares, which often featured strange landscapes and monstrous entities, as well as his fascination with ancient myths and forbidden knowledge.

Lovecraft's interest in the growing fields of archaeology and anthropology is evident in the story's references to ancient cults, unearthed artifacts, and shared human fears. While the 1920s saw a growing interest in Freud's theories, Lovecraft himself was skeptical of Freudian psychoanalysis. He dismissed Freud's dream interpretations, suggesting that his own experiences as a vivid dreamer did not align with Freudian concepts.

Lovecraft wrote "The Call of Cthulhu" during a period of growing interest in science, exploration, and the unknown. Drawing inspiration from his own vivid dreams and his fascination with the vastness of the universe and the idea that human knowledge is limited and fragile. Lovecraft's personal fears and philosophical beliefs, particularly his nihilistic worldview, heavily influenced the work. The story also exhibits elements of the era's racial and cultural concerns, which have been critiqued in modern interpretations of his work.

The Dream That Inspired It

H.P. Lovecraft was a lifelong vivid dreamer, and his subconscious often served as fertile ground for the alien, the incomprehensible, and the terrifying—elements that would become hallmarks of his fiction. Through his dreams, he glimpsed worlds and beings beyond all normal understanding, and these visions frequently found their way into his stories, none more famously than "The Call of Cthulhu".

One such dream, experienced in 1919, planted the first seed of what would become *The Horror in Clay*, the opening chapter of "The Call of Cthulhu". Lovecraft recounted this dream in two separate letters to his friend Rheinhart Kleiner, dated May 21 and December 14, 1920. In it, he found himself inside an antiquities museum in Providence, attempting to sell a strange bas-relief he had sculpted. The museum's elderly curator dismissed the piece as too modern for a collection of ancient artifacts. In response, Lovecraft recalled answering:

"Why do you say that this thing is new? The dreams of men are older than brooding Egypt or the contemplative Sphinx, or garden-girdled Babylon, and this was fashioned in my dreams."

This exchange closely mirrors a moment in "The Call of Cthulhu", where Henry Anthony Wilcox presents his own bas-relief to Professor Angell, the protagonist's uncle, seeking help in deciphering the strange hieroglyphs that came to him in a dream. Wilcox echoes Lovecraft's dream dialogue almost verbatim:

"It is new, indeed, for I made it last night in a dream of strange cities; and dreams are older than brooding Tyre or the contemplative Sphinx, or garden-girdled Babylon."

Recognizing the power of this dream, Lovecraft documented it in his "Commonplace Book", a personal journal where he jotted down story ideas and inspirations. He recorded an entry about encountering a *"gigantic piece of stone"* adorned with "curious markings," and left himself a note: *"Add good development & describe nature of bas-relief."* This dream fragment would later evolve into the grotesque bas-relief central to "The Call of Cthulhu"—a tangible connection to the ancient entity and a focal point of the protagonist's investigation into the cult surrounding Cthulhu.

In August 1925, Lovecraft expanded upon this dream-inspired idea, outlining a new story in his "Commonplace Book". He speculated about what the bas-relief might depict, refining the concept until it became the foundation of "The Call of Cthulhu". His dream of an artifact beyond human understanding grew into a story that embodied his philosophy of cosmic horror—the insignificance of humanity in the face of vast, unknowable forces lurking beyond human comprehension.

Through his meticulous documentation and creative refinement, Lovecraft transformed a fleeting dream into one of the most enduring works of weird fiction, forever intertwining his subconscious visions with the mythos he would become famous for.

Dream Elements that Influenced the Work

H.P. Lovecraft's vivid and often nightmarish dreams played a significant role in shaping "The Call of Cthulhu", influencing its characters, settings, and overarching themes of cosmic horror. One of the most direct connections between Lovecraft's dreams and the story is the mysterious bas-relief sculpture.

In a 1919 dream, Lovecraft found himself inside an antiquities museum in Providence, attempting to sell a peculiar bas-relief he had sculpted. The curator dismissed it as too modern for the museum's collection, prompting Lovecraft to argue that dreams are older than ancient civilizations, suggesting a timeless, subconscious connection to forgotten knowledge.

This dream directly inspired the character Henry Anthony Wilcox in "The Call of Cthulhu", an artist who creates a strange bas-relief and presents it to Professor Angell, claiming it was formed from his own dream visions. Lovecraft's dream dialogue is nearly identical to Wilcox's words in the story, demonstrating how deeply this personal experience influenced his fiction.

Another striking element in "The Call of Cthulhu" is the depiction of R'lyeh, the sunken city where Cthulhu lies dormant. Lovecraft frequently described dreamscapes filled with surreal, alien geometries that defied human comprehension. His fascination with non-Euclidean geometry and vast, unnatural structures is evident in his works.

R'lyeh reflects this dreamlike disorientation, with its impossibly angled architecture and oppressive, otherworldly atmosphere. The descriptions of the city in "The Call of Cthulhu" mirror Lovecraft's recurring dream imagery, reinforcing the idea that his subconscious mind served as a gateway to the cosmic horror that became a hallmark of his writing.

Dreams also function as a key narrative device in "The Call of Cthulhu", reinforcing Lovecraft's themes of cosmic horror and humanity's insignificance. Throughout the story, individuals around the world experience disturbing and prophetic dreams as Cthulhu briefly stirs from his slumber. These dreams serve as a psychic connection between humanity and the ancient entity, demonstrating that even in their sleep, people are vulnerable to incomprehensible, alien forces beyond their control.

This motif reflects Lovecraft's own beliefs about the fragility of human understanding and the terror of glimpsing hidden truths that the mind was never meant to comprehend. His personal experience with vivid dreams, which often revealed strange and terrifying worlds, provided the perfect inspiration for this concept.

Through these dream-inspired elements, Lovecraft's subconscious mind becomes a fundamental part of "The Call of Cthulhu". The bas-relief, the nightmarish city of R'lyeh, and the prophetic dreams all stem from Lovecraft's own dream experiences, transformed through his meticulous writing into some of the most iconic aspects of the story.

By intertwining his personal visions with the cosmic horror of his fiction, Lovecraft not only deepened the psychological impact of "The Call of Cthulhu" but also reinforced the central theme of his work:

that humanity is but a fleeting, fragile presence in an indifferent and incomprehensible universe.

Turning the Dream into A Novel

H.P. Lovecraft's "The Call of Cthulhu" stands as a seminal work in the genre of cosmic horror, intricately weaving elements from his vivid dreams into its narrative fabric. The process of translating these ephemeral nocturnal visions into a structured literary work presented Lovecraft with both inspiration and significant challenges.

While the dream offered a compelling starting point, Lovecraft faced the challenge of transforming this singular, dream-induced image into a comprehensive narrative. The dream provided a spark of inspiration rather than a fully formed concept.

To build upon this, Lovecraft employed his extensive knowledge of mythology, history, and his philosophical views on cosmic insignificance. He introduced the character of Henry Anthony Wilcox, an artist who, much like Lovecraft in his dream, presents a strange bas-relief to Professor Angell, claiming it was inspired by his own dream visions. This narrative device allowed Lovecraft to explore the idea of shared, otherworldly knowledge accessed through dreams.

Expanding beyond the initial dream imagery, Lovecraft crafted a multi-layered story that delved into themes of forbidden knowledge and humanity's insignificance in the vast cosmos. He wove together various accounts and perspectives, introducing elements such as the mysterious Cthulhu cult, the sunken city of R'lyeh with its non-Euclidean geometry, and the cosmic entity Cthulhu itself.

One significant challenge Lovecraft faced was articulating the ineffable—translating the indescribable nature of his dreamscapes into prose that could evoke the same sense of dread and wonder. Lovecraft leaned heavily on evocative language and sensory descriptions to create an atmosphere of dread, using phrases like "Cyclopean blocks" and "wrong geometries" to suggest rather than explicitly describe the indescribable.

However, this approach sometimes led to criticisms of verbosity and obscurity. Lovecraft himself acknowledged the difficulty of capturing the essence of his dreams, often emphasizing the limitations of language in conveying the full scope of his imaginative experiences.

Moreover, Lovecraft's philosophical stance of cosmicism—the belief in humanity's insignificance within an indifferent universe—permeated the narrative. While the initial dream provided a personal and intimate image, Lovecraft expanded it into a story that encapsulated his broader worldview.

He used the dream as a gateway to explore themes of existential dread, the fragility of sanity, and the perilous pursuit of forbidden knowledge. This expansion required a careful balance between the personal and the universal, grounding the abstract concepts in tangible imagery and characters.

Lovecraft's dreams served as a catalyst for "The Call of Cthulhu," providing a vivid image that he meticulously expanded into a complex narrative. The process involved overcoming challenges related to articulating ineffable concepts, integrating his philosophical beliefs, and crafting a story that resonated with universal themes of cosmic horror. Through this intricate melding of dream and creativity, Lovecraft transformed a fleeting nightmare into one of the most iconic works of horror fiction, ensuring its place in the pantheon of cosmic terror.

Legacy of the Dream

The legacy of Lovecraft's dream extends far beyond "The Call of Cthulhu" itself, fundamentally shaping both his career and the horror genre. The vision of Cthulhu and R'lyeh marked a pivotal shift in his writing, establishing the foundation for what would become known as the Cthulhu Mythos.

After publishing "The Call of Cthulhu," Lovecraft's work took on a more cosmic scope. His subsequent stories - including "At the Mountains of Madness" and "The Shadow over Innsmouth" - built upon themes of cosmic insignificance and unknowable horrors first crystallized in his dream. The Mythos grew to encompass other cosmic entities like Yog-Sothoth and Azathoth, each embodying the same sense of vast, alien terror.

The dream's influence rippled through the literary world. Other writers began contributing to the Mythos during Lovecraft's lifetime, expanding the shared universe he had created. After his death, authors like August Derleth and Robert E. Howard continued developing these cosmic themes, ensuring the dream's legacy lived on through new generations of writers.

In modern media, Lovecraft's dream vision has inspired countless adaptations across books, films, games, and art. Cthulhu has become an iconic figure in horror, transcending its origins to embed itself in popular culture. The themes of cosmic horror and humanity's insignificance continue to resonate, influencing works from Stephen King's novels to contemporary cosmic horror films.

The dream that sparked "The Call of Cthulhu" ultimately helped establish Lovecraft as a seminal figure in horror literature, creating a new subgenre of cosmic horror that explores humanity's place in an indifferent universe. Its impact continues to ripple through creative works today, demonstrating the lasting power of a single dream transformed into art.

Universal Themes of the Dream

The elements in Lovecraft's dream that sparked "The Call of Cthulhu" touch upon universal dream experiences many readers can relate to. The sense of discovering ancient artifacts or mysterious symbols resonates with common dream motifs of uncovering hidden knowledge or confronting the unknown.

Dreams often present us with objects or symbols we can't quite comprehend - much like Lovecraft's bas-relief. This parallels how many people experience their own dreams, where familiar objects take on strange or unsettling qualities that defy explanation. The feeling of knowing something is significant without understanding why mirrors how dream logic operates in our own nocturnal experiences.

The theme of ancient knowledge surfacing through dreams connects to the universal human experience of receiving insight through the subconscious mind. Many readers may recognize times when their own dreams seemed to tap into deeper wisdom or primal fears. Like Lovecraft's protagonist discovering cosmic truths through dreams and artifacts, we often find our dreams revealing aspects of reality we hadn't consciously considered.

The story's emphasis on shared dreams and collective unconscious experiences reflects how certain symbols and fears appear across different cultures and individuals. Readers might recognize their own encounters with archetypal images or recurring dream symbols that seem to hold deeper meaning based on their own spiritual and cultural influences.

The existential dread present in the story - the fear of forces beyond human comprehension - connects to common uncertainty about our place in the universe. Many readers can relate to dreams where they feel small and powerless against vast, incomprehensible forces, much like the characters facing Cthulhu's cosmic horror.

These universal dream elements invite readers to examine their own dream experiences and consider how their subconscious mind processes fears, discoveries, and encounters with the unknown.

Power of Dreams in Creativity

Like many creators, Lovecraft used dreams as a bridge between his conscious and unconscious mind. His nightmare of Cthulhu tapped into deep-seated fears and existential unease that he might not have accessed through pure intellectual reasoning. The dream state allowed his mind to break free from conventional thinking and imagine truly alien concepts.

In his letters, Lovecraft described how dreams helped him bypass the limitations of rational thought to envision entities and geometries that defied human comprehension. The dream-logic of R'lyeh's impossible architecture and Cthulhu's indescribable form came from a place beyond standard creative thinking.

The emotional impact of the dream - the profound sense of cosmic dread and insignificance - gave Lovecraft's writing its characteristic psychological depth. Rather than simply describing monsters, he could draw upon genuine feelings of terror and awe experienced in the dream state.

Dreams bypass our internal censors and rational filters, allowing access to deeper truths and fears that we might otherwise avoid confronting. In Lovecraft's case, his dream revealed humanity's cosmic insignificance in ways that his conscious mind might have resisted. The resulting story resonated with readers precisely because it emerged from this unfiltered well of primal terror.

By drawing directly from his dream vision, Lovecraft created something that felt both deeply personal and universally affecting. The raw emotional power of his nightmare experience translated into prose that continues to disturb and fascinate readers, demonstrating how dreams can serve as a direct conduit to our shared fears and fascinations.

Cultural Impact and Significance

When "The Call of Cthulhu" was first published in "Weird Tales" magazine in 1928, its immediate cultural impact was modest. The story was well-received within the niche readership of pulp fiction enthusiasts, who admired its originality and eerie atmosphere. For the broader public, however, the story passed largely unnoticed. Pulp magazines were often dismissed as disposable entertainment, and Lovecraft's dense prose, with its arcane vocabulary and intricate mythology, was at odds with the mainstream tastes of the time.

Yet beneath this unassuming debut, Lovecraft was quietly revolutionizing the horror genre. By abandoning traditional Gothic tropes such as ghosts and vampires, he introduced a new type of terror rooted in humanity's cosmic insignificance. The titular Cthulhu—a godlike, alien entity—was not just a monster but a harbinger of existential dread. Lovecraft's vision of the universe as an incomprehensibly vast, indifferent expanse laid the foundation for what would come to be known as cosmic horror.

His creation of the Cthulhu Mythos—a shared universe of interconnected stories and entities—was groundbreaking. This approach not only influenced literary successors like Neil Gaiman but also inspired the interconnected storytelling of modern franchises, from superhero universes to multimedia adaptations.

Beyond literature, "The Call of Cthulhu" left an indelible mark on popular culture, with the entity of Cthulhu evolving into a cultural icon. Cthulhu has appeared in various forms of media, including tabletop role-playing games, music, and merchandise.

The tabletop role-playing game "Call of Cthulhu," released in 1981, was instrumental in popularizing Lovecraft's mythos. Designed by Sandy Petersen, the game emphasized investigation and psychological horror over combat, aligning closely with Lovecraft's themes of cosmic dread. This innovative approach attracted a wide audience and introduced many to Lovecraft's work.

In music, numerous metal bands have drawn inspiration from Lovecraft's creations, incorporating references to Cthulhu and other elements of the mythos into their lyrics and themes. For example, Metallica's instrumental track "The Call of Ktulu" and their song "The Thing That Should Not Be" are directly influenced by Lovecraft's writings.

Additionally, Cthulhu has been adapted into various forms of merchandise, including plush toys, further cementing its place in popular culture. This widespread presence underscores the enduring impact of Lovecraft's creation, which continues to captivate and inspire audiences across different media.

Guillermo del Toro's cinematic creatures often reflect Lovecraftian influences, as do countless depictions of hybrid horrors in modern film and television. The visual and thematic language of Lovecraft's cosmic horror continues to permeate storytelling across media.

Perhaps "The Call of Cthulhu's" most enduring contribution is its redefinition of horror itself. Lovecraft shifted the genre's focus from familiar supernatural threats to the unsettling vastness of the unknown. This reorientation transformed horror into a vehicle for exploring existential fears—the fragility of the human mind, the limits of comprehension, and the insignificance of humanity in an uncaring cosmos. This approach influenced subsequent writers.

Stephen King has acknowledged Lovecraft's profound influence on the horror genre, stating that Lovecraft "opened a door that can't be closed." Clive Barker's exploration of otherworldly realms reflects a conceptual alignment with Lovecraftian themes.

At the time of its publication, Lovecraft's masterpiece dwelled in the shadows of pulp fiction, its significance overlooked by mainstream audiences. But over the decades, its influence grew, expanding far beyond its humble beginnings. Today, "The Call of Cthulhu" stands as a cornerstone of modern horror, its tentacles extending into literature, music, gaming, and visual art. It is a testament to how even the quietest ripples in literary history can grow into tidal waves of cultural transformation.

Chapter 4

The Shining
by Stephen King

Stephen King published "The Shining" in 1977, marking his third published novel after "Carrie" (1974) and "'Salem's Lot" (1975). At the time of its publication, King was 29 years old, firmly establishing himself as a leading voice in modern horror fiction.

During this period, King was living with his wife, Tabitha King, and their two children, Naomi and Joseph (who would later become the writer Joe Hill). The family had moved from Maine to Boulder, Colorado, in the early 1970s. They lived there for about a year, during which King found inspiration for "The Shining". Afterward, they returned to Maine, where King would remain for most of his career.

While King was gaining success as a writer, he was also battling personal demons, particularly alcoholism and drug abuse, issues that would persist for years. He has admitted that "The Shining" was partially autobiographical, reflecting his growing fears about his own alcoholism and its potential effect on his family. The character of Jack Torrance, an aspiring writer struggling with alcohol and rage, mirrored some of King's own fears about himself.

Financially, King was doing much better than in the early years when he and Tabitha struggled to make ends meet. The success of "Carrie" had allowed him to transition into full-time writing, and the success of "Salem's Lot" further cemented his career.

During this time, King was corresponding with several established authors in the horror and fantasy genre, including Peter Straub, whom he would later collaborate with on "The Talisman" (1984). King was also heavily influenced by the works of Shirley Jackson, particularly her novel "The Haunting of Hill House" (1959), which shaped his approach to haunted house fiction. Another influence included Richard Matheson, particularly his novel "Hell House".

The title "The Shining" was inspired by John Lennon's song "Instant Karma!", which contains the line: *"We all shine on...like the moon and the stars and the sun."* King liked the idea of people possessing a supernatural "shine" or psychic ability, which became a central theme in the novel, particularly through the young protagonist, Danny Torrance.

Synopsis of the Storyline

"The Shining" is a psychological horror novel that follows the story of Jack Torrance, a struggling writer and recovering alcoholic, who takes a job as the winter caretaker of the isolated Overlook Hotel in Colorado. Hoping to rebuild his life and reconnect with his family, Jack moves into the hotel with his wife, Wendy, and their five-year-old son, Danny. However, the Overlook is no ordinary hotel—it harbors a sinister presence that begins to unravel the fragile stability of the Torrance family.

Danny Torrance possesses a psychic ability known as "the shining," which allows him to perceive the hotel's dark history and its malevolent spirits. Early on, Danny is warned by Dick Hallorann, the Overlook's chef and a fellow "shiner," to avoid Room 217 and to contact him psychically if he ever needs help. Despite this warning, Danny becomes increasingly aware of the hotel's horrific past, including violent deaths and dark secrets tied to previous guests and caretakers.

As the harsh winter sets in, the Torrances become cut off from the outside world, and Jack begins to succumb to the Overlook's influence. Already haunted by his own demons—his struggle with alcoholism, a history of abusive behavior, and frustration over his stalled writing career—Jack becomes a prime target for the hotel's evil forces. They manipulate him, pushing him to madness and urging him to murder his family, as the hotel's previous caretaker, Delbert Grady, had done.

Wendy and Danny, meanwhile, fight to survive Jack's increasingly erratic and violent behavior. Danny uses his psychic abilities to understand the hotel's motivations and to seek help. Wendy, initially hoping to protect her son while salvaging their fractured family, realizes she must take drastic action to escape the growing danger.

The novel reaches its climax as Jack, fully possessed by the Overlook, turns on his family in a terrifying attempt to kill them. Jack pursues Danny through the hotel, Danny confronts his father by calling out to him, which momentarily breaks the hotel's hold on Jack. This brief moment of clarity allows Jack to tell Danny to run away before the hotel's influence regains control. Jack then succumbs to the hotel's possession, leading to his demise.

Meanwhile, Wendy and Danny attempt to flee, aided by Hallorann, who returns to the Overlook after receiving Danny's psychic call for help. The Overlook's evil plans are ultimately thwarted when Jack loses control, and the hotel's malfunctioning boiler explodes, destroying the building and killing Jack.

Wendy and Danny escape, with Hallorann helping them to safety. The novel ends with the surviving characters seeking to rebuild their lives, though Danny's shining abilities and the trauma of their experience suggest that the horrors of the Overlook will continue to resonate.

Context of Creation

In the fall of 1974, following the success of "Carrie", Stephen King was navigating the challenges of newfound fame and the pressures of supporting his family. During this time, he and his wife, Tabitha, stayed at The Stanley Hotel in Colorado, an experience that profoundly influenced the creation of "The Shining".

The Kings arrived at the Stanley Hotel in Estes Park, Colorado as its final guests before its seasonal closure. The hotel's eerie desolation and decaying grandeur deeply resonated with King's creative instincts. Wandering the empty corridors of the vast, Victorian-style building, King was struck by the contradictions of its isolation and opulence.

That night, he experienced a vivid dream of his son running terrified through the hotel's hallways, pursued by a living fire hose. The haunting imagery and the hotel's ambiance planted the seeds for what would become "The Shining".

Upon returning home, King began writing "The Shining", immersing himself in the project over the subsequent months. The novel was published on January 28, 1977, marking King's third published work and his first hardcover bestseller. This success firmly established him as a leading figure in the horror genre.

The novel reflected both King's personal struggles and the broader societal concerns of the 1970s. King poured his own fears about alcoholism, failure, and the pressures of family life into the character of Jack Torrance.

Jack's descent into madness and violence mirrored King's battle with addiction and his terror at the potential for self-destruction. These personal themes found a larger context in the cultural shifts of the era.

The 1970s were marked by economic instability, rising divorce rates, and evolving family dynamics, all of which influenced "The Shining". Jack Torrance's desperate need for a job as the caretaker of the Overlook Hotel reflected the financial pressures of the time, while Wendy Torrance's struggles with her role as a wife and mother highlighted the disillusionment many felt with traditional family structures.

The aftermath of the Vietnam War further shaped the novel's themes of isolation and paranoia. The Overlook Hotel, with its remote location and claustrophobic atmosphere, became a chilling metaphor for the sense of emotional and political disconnect that many Americans felt during the decade.

Society's fascination with the supernatural and occult in the 1970s also influenced the story. The era saw a growing interest in parapsychology and the occult, which made Danny Torrance's psychic abilities both timely and compelling for readers.

At the same time, the novel's exploration of addiction and recovery reflected an evolving understanding of alcoholism. The 1970s marked a shift in public awareness of addiction as a disease rather than a moral failing, and Jack Torrance's struggles mirrored both King's personal experience and society's changing attitudes.

By blending his own fears and struggles with the cultural concerns of the 1970s, Stephen King created a deeply personal and resonant story in "The Shining". The novel's exploration of familial dysfunction, addiction, and societal unease struck a chord with readers, solidifying King's place as one of the defining voices of modern horror.

The Dream that Inspired It

King's dream at the Stanley Hotel emerged from a perfect storm of circumstances while him and his wife stayed at the Stanley Hotel. They found themselves the only guests in the expansive, eerie establishment. That evening, they dined alone in the grand but empty dining room, accompanied by canned orchestral music echoing through the deserted halls.

In his own words, King remarked:

"The hotel staff were just getting ready to close for the season, and we found ourselves the only guests in the place— with all those long, empty corridors. Except for our table all the chairs were up on the tables. So the music is echoing down the hall, and, I mean, it was like God had put me there to hear that and see those things."

After dinner, while Tabitha retired for the night, King wandered the hotel's vacant corridors, the sound of his footsteps reverberating through the empty halls. The hotel's grandeur, coupled with its decay—peeling wallpaper, creaking floorboards, and the palpable weight of its history—seeped into his subconscious. Eventually, he returned to their room, numbered 217, and fell asleep.

That night, King experienced a vivid nightmare that would become the foundation of "The Shining":

"I dreamed of my three-year-old son running through the corridors, looking back over his shoulder, eyes wide, screaming. He was being chased by a fire-hose. I woke up with a tremendous jerk, sweating all over, within an inch of falling out of bed. I got up, lit a cigarette, sat in a chair looking out the window at the Rockies, and by the time the cigarette was done, I had the bones of the book firmly set in my mind."

Unable to return to sleep, King lit a cigarette to calm his nerves, he felt the framework of "The Shining" crystallize in his mind—not just the plot, but the deeper themes of isolation, family, and a father's descent into madness. The hotel, its unsettling ambiance, and his nightmare coalesced into a narrative rich with psychological depth.

The dream tapped into King's deepest fears about himself as a father. He later recognized that "The Shining" was heavily influenced by his personal struggles with alcoholism and his fears of failing his family. The character of Jack Torrance embodies these themes, grappling with addiction and the potential disintegration of his family. King described the act of writing the novel as "a kind of self-psychoanalysis," helping him confront and understand his own inner demons.

This intense, personal experience and the Stanley Hotel's haunting atmosphere became the catalyst for "The Shining". The novel not only reflects King's own fears and struggles but also explores universal themes of creativity, isolation, and self-destruction, making it one of his most psychologically profound works.

Dream Elements that Influenced the Work

Stephen King's vivid nightmare during his stay at the Stanley Hotel became the foundation for many of the key characters, scenes, and themes in "The Shining". This dream, combined with the eerie ambiance of the nearly deserted hotel and King's own personal struggles, provided the raw material for one of his most psychologically profound works. Central to the novel's creation were the dream's symbolic elements, which tapped into King's deepest fears and translated into a haunting narrative of isolation, madness, and supernatural terror.

One of the most memorable scenes in the novel—Danny's encounter with an animated fire hose—drew directly from King's nightmare. Danny's vulnerability mirrors the fear King felt seeing his son in peril within the dream, highlighting the fragility of childhood and the looming threats that can arise from forces beyond a parent's control.

This vulnerability becomes a central theme in the novel, as Danny represents innocence threatened by malevolent forces. This moment also illustrates how mundane objects can become sources of terror under the Overlook's influence, reflecting the novel's recurring motif of distorted reality. The fire hose serves as a symbol of how seemingly ordinary threats can become insurmountable when magnified by fear and supernatural manipulation.

King's dream tapped into his profound angst about fatherhood. Watching his son in mortal danger in the dream forced King to confront his fear of failing as a parent and, worse, becoming a danger to his own family.

These fears were weaved into the character of Jack Torrance, whose descent into madness also finds its roots in King's nightmare. The fire hose, a symbol of an uncontrollable menace in the dream, parallels Jack's struggles with alcoholism, anger, and creative frustration.

King channeled his own fears about his temper and addiction into Jack's character, crafting a tragic arc that reflects the destructive potential of unchecked personal demons. Jack's transformation from a struggling father to a possessed antagonist underscores themes of self-destruction and the harm one's flaws can inflict on loved ones.

The setting of the Stanley Hotel heavily influenced the Overlook Hotel's predatory nature in the novel. The Stanley's empty corridors, decaying grandeur, and the weight of its history were transformed into the Overlook's sinister character.

King developed the Overlook into more than just a backdrop; it became a living entity with its own desires and will, manipulating its inhabitants and amplifying their weaknesses. The way sound echoed through vacant hallways, shadows played in abandoned spaces, and the overwhelming sense of isolation all stemmed from King's experience at the Stanley.

Finally, the dream and its setting reinforced the theme of isolation, a cornerstone of "The Shining". The empty, desolate corridors of the Stanley Hotel left King with a sense of eerie solitude, which became a defining element of the Overlook.

The Torrance family's physical isolation during the winter mirrors their emotional disconnection, creating fertile ground for the Overlook's malevolence to take hold. Isolation amplifies the characters' vulnerabilities, allowing both personal flaws and supernatural forces to fester and grow.

By weaving the elements of his nightmare into the novel, King created a chilling narrative that feels both intensely personal and universally resonant. The dream's emotional intensity—its pursuit, fear, and helplessness—provided the framework for "The Shining's" complex characters, haunting atmosphere, and timeless themes of vulnerability, family, and the destructive power of isolation and fear.

Turning the Dream into A Novel

Stephen King's dream at the Stanley Hotel was the spark of inspiration that ultimately led to "The Shining". Building upon this initial vision,

King wrote the first draft in less than four months, delving into themes of alcoholism, self-destruction, and the complexities of family dynamics.

The vivid image of King's young son running in fear through endless corridors, pursued by a living fire hose, provided the emotional core of the story but lacked the complexity and narrative structure required for a full-length book. To expand this raw material into a resonant work of art, King had to craft rich characters, layered themes, and a vivid setting, all while addressing his own personal struggles.

One of the key challenges was balancing the psychological and supernatural elements of the story. King's dream reflected his personal fears—parental failure, addiction, and loss of control—but these internal struggles needed to coexist with the external malevolence of the Overlook Hotel.

King carefully developed Jack Torrance's psychological deterioration in tandem with the supernatural influence of the hotel, ensuring that the novel remained emotionally grounded while amplifying its horror. Writing Jack's character was especially difficult for King, as it forced him to confront his own struggles with alcohol and anger. Jack's descent into madness and eventual transformation into a weapon of the hotel mirrored King's fears of his own destructive tendencies and their potential impact on his family.

The dream also provided little in terms of narrative complexity, requiring King to expand its scope and build a rich world around its core imagery. He infused the Overlook Hotel with a malevolent presence, turning it into more than just a setting.

Layers of backstory—tragic events, ghostly manifestations, and the hotel's predatory intent—were added to create a space that actively manipulated its inhabitants. This transformation of the Stanley Hotel's eerie isolation into the Overlook's sinister grandeur required significant world-building, including details about its architecture, its long history of tragedy, and its ability to exploit the weaknesses of its guests.

At the heart of the novel, King needed to craft a believable family dynamic to heighten the emotional stakes. The dream centered on a child in peril, which inspired the character of Danny Torrance and his psychic abilities, or "the shining." This gift made Danny both a victim of the Overlook's supernatural forces and a critical force for survival.

Wendy Torrance's role also expanded as King explored the resilience required to protect one's family while coping with the instability of an unraveling partner. These characters became deeply intertwined with King's personal fears about fatherhood, addiction, and the pressures of creative failure.

King's writing process, undertaken at his home in Boulder, Colorado, involved channeling the Stanley Hotel's eerie ambiance into the fictional Overlook. He maintained the dream's claustrophobic intensity by isolating the Torrance family during the Colorado winter, using the snowbound hotel as a natural barrier that trapped them with the growing menace.

The Overlook's creeping dread, seen in details like the hedge animals, the woman in Room 217, and the ominous masked ball, grew from King's desire to create a place where reality itself became unreliable.

The process of writing "The Shining" also forced King to expand the dream's primal terror into a broader meditation on themes of isolation, family bonds under pressure, and human vulnerability. The economic uncertainties and shifting family dynamics of the 1970s provided additional layers of resonance.

Through disciplined writing and introspection, King transformed his nightmare into a multi-dimensional narrative that explores not only supernatural horror but also the human capacity for destruction and redemption. His ability to turn a single dream into a timeless and layered work of art is a testament to his creative genius.

Legacy of the Dream

Stephen King's 1974 stay at the Stanley Hotel in Estes Park, Colorado, and the vivid nightmare he experienced there provided the foundation for "The Shining", one of the most celebrated horror novels of all time. The dream—of his young son running in terror through the hotel's corridors, pursued by a fire hose—was the spark that ignited King's vision for the novel. However, "The Shining's" impact extends far beyond that single night of inspiration, shaping King's career, influencing his subsequent works, and leaving an indelible mark on popular culture.

When "The Shining" was published in 1977, King had already found success with "Carrie" (1974) and "Salem's Lot" (1975). However, "The Shining" was his first hardcover bestseller and significantly elevated his standing in the literary world. The novel demonstrated his ability to merge psychological depth with supernatural horror, establishing him as a master of the genre. The commercial and critical success of "The Shining" helped solidify his reputation, paving the way for future works such as "The Stand" (1978) and "It" (1986).

"The Shining" also marked a turning point in King's thematic exploration of personal demons, particularly alcoholism, which deeply influenced the characterization of Jack Torrance. This deeply personal storytelling became a hallmark of King's work, reappearing in novels such as "Doctor Sleep" (2013)—the sequel to "The Shining", which more explicitly examines addiction and recovery. The novel's themes of isolation, domestic tension, and psychological breakdown became recurring motifs in King's later books, reinforcing his reputation as an author who blended personal fears with universal horror.

The novel's legacy expanded with Stanley Kubrick's 1980 film adaptation of "The Shining", which, despite King's well-documented disdain for its deviations from the book, propelled the story into mainstream consciousness. The eerie, isolated setting of the Overlook Hotel, the descent of Jack Torrance into madness, and the supernatural horror elements became cultural touchstones, inspiring countless homages in literature, film, and television. The book also led to a successful sequel, "Doctor Sleep", and its 2019 film adaptation, further extending the story's influence.

The blend of supernatural horror and psychological depth that "The Shining" perfected became a defining feature of King's career. Elements of haunted spaces and malevolent forces manipulating human weakness appear in later works such as "Bag of Bones" (1998), "Duma Key" (2008), and "Revival" (2014). His ability to take a singular, personal moment of inspiration—a dream of fear and helplessness—and turn it into a deeply layered narrative became a blueprint for his storytelling approach.

Ultimately, King's dream at the Stanley Hotel was more than a creative spark—it was a foundational moment that shaped the trajectory of his literary career, deepened his exploration of psychological horror, and left an indelible mark on popular culture.

Universal Themes of the Dream

Stephen King's dream at the Stanley Hotel, is deeply connected to universal themes that resonate with readers and viewers on a psychological and emotional level. The dream's imagery and the resulting novel explore timeless human concerns such as fear of failure, vulnerability, isolation, and the loss of control—all of which are common in both waking life and the symbolic realm of dreams.

By drawing on these universal themes, King created a story that allows audiences to relate the eerie and unsettling elements of "The Shining" to their own subconscious experiences and life challenges.

Dreams often feature symbolic representations of emotions, fears, and desires, and King's nightmare was no exception. The corridors of the Overlook Hotel evoke feelings of entrapment and confusion, a common theme in dreams where individuals feel lost or unable to find their way. This mirrors real-life fears of being trapped in circumstances beyond one's control, whether in relationships, careers, or personal struggles.

The image of King's son being chased by a living fire hose symbolizes the fear of an inescapable threat, another frequent motif in dreams. This pursuit can represent unresolved fears or pressures, such as the challenges of protecting loved ones, managing personal flaws, or escaping harmful influences. Similarly, the fire hose coming to life reflects the dreamlike tendency for ordinary objects to take on sinister meanings, speaking to a universal fear of the familiar becoming dangerous and the unpredictability of life's challenges.

The setting of the Overlook Hotel reinforces feelings of loneliness and abandonment, resonating with those who have experienced physical or emotional disconnection. Jack Torrance's descent into madness and the Overlook's manipulation of reality highlight the fear of losing autonomy, a theme often tied to troubles with addiction, mental health, and personal identity.

Readers and viewers might see echoes of their own dreams in "The Shining's" surreal and symbolic elements. Many dreams feature disorienting settings, shifting realities, or scenarios where the dreamer feels powerless—qualities that are central to the Overlook Hotel and its impact on the Torrance family.

The novel's dreamlike logic, where time and space are fluid and ordinary objects become menacing, mirrors the unpredictable nature of dreams. Jack Torrance's struggle with his inner demons might remind readers of moments when they felt overwhelmed by their own emotions or behaviors.

Similarly, Danny Torrance's psychic awareness, or "shining," represents the heightened sensitivity that individuals often experience in dreams, where they perceive dangers or truths that remain hidden in waking life. These connections make "The Shining" not only a gripping horror story but also a profound exploration of the human psyche.

Power of Dreams in Creativity

King's nightmare at the Stanley Hotel demonstrates the raw creative power that dreams can unlock. In that vulnerable state between sleep and consciousness, his mind assembled the building blocks of what would become "The Shining" - the endless corridors, the haunted fire hose, and the deep sense of isolation that permeates the novel.

Dreams tap into our deepest fears and desires, bypassing conscious filters to reveal psychological truths. For King, the Stanley Hotel dream exposed his anxieties about fatherhood, addiction, and creative isolation. These elements emerged organically in his sleep, allowing him to explore them through fiction without the constraints of waking logic.

The transformation of dream imagery into coherent narrative shows how the creative mind processes unconscious material. King took the fragmentary scenes and emotions from his nightmare and wove them into a complex story. The Overlook Hotel became more than just a setting - it evolved into a character itself, embodying the malevolent forces that threaten to tear families apart.

The lasting impact of King's dream-inspired work proves how powerful these nocturnal visions can be. By trusting his subconscious mind to guide the story's development, he created characters and situations that feel authentic despite their supernatural elements. The primal fears and family dynamics at the heart of "The Shining" emerged from that initial dream state, giving the novel its psychological depth.

For creative individuals, King's experience highlights the value of paying attention to dreams. These nighttime narratives can provide unique perspectives and unexpected connections that conscious thinking might miss. "The Shining" stands as testament to how a single dream can spark a masterwork when the creator remains open to its possibilities and willing to explore its darker implications.

Cultural Impact and Significance

Stephen King's "The Shining" made a significant cultural impact upon its release in 1977 and has continued to shape the landscape of horror and psychological storytelling. The novel was well-received by both the general public and critics, cementing King's reputation as a master of the horror genre.

Its blend of supernatural elements, psychological depth, and universal themes of family, isolation, and vulnerability resonated deeply with readers, setting it apart from traditional horror works of the time. The novel's success also reflected a broader cultural fascination with darker, more introspective narratives during the 1970s, a period marked by societal upheaval and a growing appetite for stories that explored personal and collective fears.

At the time of its publication, "The Shining" was celebrated for elevating horror beyond simple scares. Readers and critics praised its complex characters, particularly Jack Torrance, whose descent into madness struck a chord with audiences familiar with the struggles of addiction and familial dysfunction.

The novel tapped into the zeitgeist of the 1970s, a decade defined by economic uncertainty, shifting family dynamics, and growing awareness of mental health and addiction issues. The Torrance family's isolation in the Overlook Hotel mirrored broader societal fears of disconnection and alienation, making the story feel both personal and universal.

The general public was captivated by King's ability to blend supernatural horror with psychological realism, and "The Shining" became a bestseller, solidifying King's position as a major literary figure. Its success helped expand the horror genre's appeal to a wider audience and paved the way for horror to be taken more seriously as a literary form, opening doors for stories that explored complex themes through the lens of fear and suspense.

"The Shining" also had a profound influence on other genres, inspiring creators in literature, film, and television to adopt similar approaches to storytelling. Its psychological depth and character-driven narrative encouraged horror writers to explore the internal lives of their characters rather than relying solely on external threats.

The novel's emphasis on familial relationships and emotional vulnerability introduced a level of complexity that redefined the expectations of the genre. In film, Stanley Kubrick's 1980 adaptation brought "The Shining" to an even larger audience, despite King's dissatisfaction with Kubrick's interpretation. The iconic quote "Here's Johnny!" is one of the most memorable lines in film history.

The film's haunting visuals, ambiguous storytelling, and psychological terror set a new standard for horror cinema, influencing a wave of films that prioritized atmosphere and character over gore. Movies such as "Poltergeist" (1982) and "The Others" (2001) echoed themes of haunted spaces and familial conflict that were central to "The Shining".

The Stanley Hotel in Estes Park, Colorado, which inspired Stephen King's "The Shining", continues to draw visitors from all over the world, many of whom are eager to experience the eerie atmosphere that influenced the novel. In fact, one of the most popular draws for visitors is Room 217, which is often referred to as "The Stephen King Room."

In addition to Room 217, the Stanley Hotel offers ghost tours that highlight the haunted history of the property. The hotel has been featured in numerous paranormal investigations, documentaries, and other media, solidifying its place as a hub for horror enthusiasts.

Beyond horror, "The Shining's" exploration of isolation and madness had ripple effects across other genres. Psychological thrillers, dramas, and even science fiction began incorporating elements of suspense and internal conflict reminiscent of King's work.

The novel's depiction of a malevolent setting—the Overlook Hotel—popularized the concept of environments that act as active, almost sentient antagonists, a trope that has since appeared in genres ranging from fantasy to dystopian fiction.

The general public was fascinated by "The Shining's" ability to blend terror with relatability. Its exploration of addiction, family breakdown, and the fragility of sanity struck a nerve with readers, many of whom found the Torrance family's struggles as compelling as the supernatural elements of the story. While the novel was celebrated as a masterpiece of horror, it also appealed to readers who might not typically engage with the genre due to its emotional depth and literary quality.

Overall, "The Shining" not only cemented Stephen King's place as one of the greatest horror writers of all time but also left an indelible mark on popular culture. It redefined the boundaries of horror, paving the way for more introspective and character-driven narratives, and its influence can still be felt across a wide range of creative works.

Chapter 5

Misery
by Stephen King

In 1987, Stephen King unleashed "Misery" upon the world, a claustrophobic psychological thriller that marked a departure from his supernatural horror roots. By this time, King was at the peak of his career, having already published literary sensations like "Carrie" (1974), "The Shining" (1977), and "It" (1986), which solidified his reputation as a master of horror and suspense.

King was living in Bangor, Maine, a location that would later serve as the inspiration for many of the towns in his novels. Despite his fame and financial success, King was facing significant personal challenges when he wrote "Misery".

He was struggling with substance abuse, particularly alcohol and cocaine, and had recently entered a period of sobriety around the time he worked on the novel. This struggle with addiction, alongside his rocky relationship with fame, heavily influenced the themes of "Misery", particularly the notion of being trapped by one's own success and being at the mercy of an obsessive and controlling force, which mirrored his own struggles with his personal demons.

King's family life at the time was stable. He was married to his wife, Tabitha King. The couple had three children: Naomi, Joe, and Owen. Tabitha, a writer herself, had a supportive role in his career, and her presence in his life was an anchor during his battles with addiction and fame.

The title "Misery" itself reflects the central theme of the novel—the intense suffering that Paul Sheldon endures at the hands of Annie Wilkes. For Stephen King, the character of Annie Wilkes served as a metaphor for his own struggles with addiction, particularly his battle with cocaine. King famously stated, "Annie was my drug problem, and she was my number-one fan." In this sense, Wilkes represents the overwhelming and destructive force of addiction, mirroring the way it can consume and control an individual.

King also revealed that part of the inspiration for "Misery" came from a lesser-known short story by Evelyn Waugh, titled "The Man Who Loved Dickens." Waugh's story centers on a man obsessed with the works of Charles Dickens to the point of fanaticism, much like Annie's obsession with Paul Sheldon's novels. This story was an important influence on King's development of the character of Annie, whose unhealthy devotion to Sheldon forces him into a terrifying captivity.

King's own experiences as a writer also influenced the creation of "Misery". At the time, he was navigating the pressure of being a highly successful author and the overwhelming expectations placed upon him by his readers. The idea of being trapped by the demands of fans and the creative process is reflected in Paul Sheldon's plight, offering a chilling and introspective look at the cost of fame.

Despite these struggles, he produced one of his most iconic works, combining his literary skills with his personal experiences to create a gripping psychological horror novel.

Synopsis of the Storyline

"Misery" tells the story of Paul Sheldon, a successful novelist known for his series of historical romance novels featuring the character Misery Chastain. After finishing the final book in the series, "Misery's Child", in which he kills off Misery, Paul is eager to branch out to other genres.

He finishes a new manuscript, "Fast Cars", hoping to gain serious literary acclaim. Despite his agent's concerns about ending the Misery series, Paul feels it was necessary to avoid being typecast as a romance writer.

While in seclusion at a cabin near Sidewinder, Colorado, Paul celebrates completing "Fast Cars" with champagne. On a drunken impulse, he decides to drive to California but is caught in a blizzard, causing his car to crash.

Paul is rescued by Annie Wilkes, a former nurse, who brings him to her secluded home. Paul is bedridden with broken legs and dependent on Novril, an addictive painkiller that Annie controls.

Annie, claiming to be Paul's "number one fan," reads "Misery's Child" and becomes enraged when she discovers Paul killed off Misery. She forces him to burn the "Fast Cars" manuscript and demands that he write a new Misery novel, "Misery's Return", bringing the character back to life.

Paul reluctantly agrees and begins writing, using a broken typewriter that lacks the letter "N." Annie insists on reading each chapter and makes numerous demands, causing Paul further distress.

As Paul writes, he realizes Annie is mentally unstable and capable of extreme violence. He eventually discovers through a scrapbook that

Annie is a serial killer who was never convicted of her crimes. She has murdered several people, including infants and elderly patients.

To punish Paul for his efforts to escape, Annie brutally amputates his foot with an axe and cauterizes the wound with a blowtorch. She continues to torment him, even cutting off his thumb when Paul complains about the broken keys on the typewriter.

As Paul works on the novel, he gains small moments of strength and courage, using the heavy typewriter to build his upper body. One day, while escaping his room to find more painkillers, he finds a kitchen knife and plans to kill Annie. However, she catches him, and to punish him further, she locks him in the basement.

A state trooper arrives searching for Paul, but Annie kills him with a riding lawnmower and hides his body. The trooper's disappearance draws attention, and Annie begins to fear Paul might escape.

Finally, Paul finishes "Misery's Return" and, knowing Annie will want to celebrate, tricks her into giving him a match. He sets the manuscript on fire, and when Annie attempts to save it, Paul attacks her with the typewriter. After a violent struggle, Paul knocks Annie unconscious. He is later rescued by two cops, who find Annie dead in her barn from a blow to the head.

Back in New York, "Misery's Return" is a massive success. Paul's agent urges him to write a nonfiction account of his ordeal, but Paul refuses, fearing he would fictionalize the events. Though he has a prosthetic foot and has returned to writing, he suffers from nightmares, hallucinations, and writer's block. One day, while out shopping, Paul has an odd encounter that sparks his creativity, and he begins writing again, rediscovering his muse despite the lingering trauma of his captivity.

Context of Creation

"Misery" was conceived during a complex and turbulent period in Stephen King's life, marked by both professional success and personal struggles. In the mid-1980s, King was at the height of his career, having gained widespread recognition for his previous works.

However, his success came with its own pressures, particularly the burden of managing fame while grappling with his personal demons, including addiction to alcohol and cocaine. These internal battles, combined with the growing demands of his audience, served as the backdrop for "Misery".

The novel reflects King's fears of being trapped by his success and the suffocating expectations placed on him as a writer, which is mirrored in the struggles of Paul Sheldon, the protagonist, who faces entrapment both physically and creatively.

The 1980s also saw a rise in fan culture, with audiences becoming more vocal and obsessive, leading to what would later be termed "stalker culture." This cultural shift deeply influenced the novel, as King channeled his own experiences with the darker side of fame into the disturbing relationship between Paul Sheldon and Annie Wilkes.

Annie, a seemingly sweet and harmless fan, transforms into an unhinged captor, embodying the dangers of obsessive fandom and the blurred line between admiration and possession. This dynamic reflects the growing tension between creators and their increasingly demanding audiences, which King experienced firsthand.

"Misery" was also written during a time when psychological thrillers were gaining prominence in horror literature, shifting away from supernatural elements to explore more intimate, character-driven horror. The novel's confined setting in a remote Colorado farmhouse, combined with its focus on psychological torture, resonates with the era's growing interest in human monsters and psychological horror.

The absence of modern technology—like cell phones and the internet—adds to the believability of Paul's predicament, as he is isolated in a way that feels grounded in the pre-internet age. The typewriter, a symbol of the writer's craft, serves as both a tool and a weapon in Paul's struggle, emphasizing the period's mechanical, as opposed to digital, writing methods.

King's struggles with addiction and the tension between his creative freedom and the expectations of his audience are reflected in "Misery's" themes of entrapment, obsession, and the dark side of fame. Annie Wilkes embodies the hidden danger beneath a seemingly ordinary and peaceful setting, reflecting the 1980s horror trend of contrasting outward appearances with concealed menace.

This theme, which was common in the era's horror, reflects societal concerns about the dangers that could lie beneath the surface of everyday life. Ultimately, "Misery" emerged from a period of both triumph and turmoil, capturing King's personal fears about being pigeonholed as a genre writer while also exploring the growing tensions between artists and their increasingly demanding audiences. It remains one of King's most personal and enduring works.

The Dream that Inspired It

Stephen King's novel "Misery" was significantly inspired by a vivid nightmare he experienced during a transatlantic flight to London. In his memoir "On Writing: A Memoir of the Craft", King recounts falling asleep on the plane and dreaming about a popular writer who becomes captive to a psychotic fan living on a remote farm. This fan even had a pet pig named Misery, after the protagonist of the author's romance series.

Upon waking, King jotted down the idea on an American Airlines cocktail napkin to ensure he wouldn't forget it:

"She speaks earnestly but never quite makes eye contact. A big woman and solid all through; she is an absence of hiatus. 'I wasn't trying to be funny in a mean way when I named my pig Misery, no sir. Please don't think that. No, I named her in the spirit of fan love, which is the purest love there is. You should be flattered.'"

In a subsequent interview King elaborated more on his dream:

"Like the ideas for some of my other novels, that came to me in a dream. In fact, it happened when I was on Concord, flying over here, to Brown's [a hotel in England]. I fell asleep on the plane and dreamt about a woman who held a writer prisoner and killed him, skinned him, fed the remains to her pig and bound his novel in human skin. His skin, the writer's skin. I said to myself, 'I have to write this story.' Of course, the plot changed quite a bit in the telling. But I wrote the first forty or fifty pages right on the landing here, between the ground floor and the first floor of the hotel."

During their stay at Brown's Hotel in London, Stephen King and his wife, Tabitha, found themselves in a historic setting where King began writing "Misery". He drafted sixteen pages in a steno notebook while working at a desk once used by Rudyard Kipling—the very desk where Kipling had suffered a fatal stroke.

Initially, King estimated the novel would be around 30,000 words, but it ultimately expanded to 370 pages. The book's working title was "The Annie Wilkes Edition". Reflecting on his writing process, King later admitted that he had first envisioned a much darker ending, where

Annie Wilkes would force Paul Sheldon to write a novel, only to bind it using his own skin.

When commenting on why he chose not to go that route, King said:

"... it would have made a pretty good story (not such a good novel, however; no one likes to root for a guy over the course of three hundred pages only to discover that between chapters sixteen and seventeen the pig ate him), but that wasn't the way things eventually went. Paul Sheldon turned out to be a good deal more resourceful than I initially thought, and his efforts to play Scheherazade and save his life gave me a chance to say some things about the redemptive power of writing that I had long felt but never articulated. Annie also turned out to be more complex than I'd first imagined her, and she was great fun to write about ..."

Beyond the nightmare, King has acknowledged that "Misery" reflects his personal struggles with addiction. He stated, "Annie was my drug problem, and she was my number-one fan. God, she never wanted to leave." This metaphor illustrates how his battle with substance abuse felt like being held captive by an unrelenting force, much like the protagonist, Paul Sheldon, is imprisoned by Annie Wilkes.

King also intended "Misery" to explore the pressures of fame and the sometimes toxic relationship between authors and their fans. He once recounted an encounter with a fan named Mark Chapman, who persistently sought his autograph. Chapman later gained infamy for murdering John Lennon. This incident highlighted for King the unsettling nature of obsessive fandom, a theme central to "Misery".

King has described how the dream tapped into his own apprehensions about fame and artistic freedom. In interviews, he's connected Annie Wilkes' character to the metaphorical trap many successful authors face - the pressure to continue writing what their readers demand rather than exploring new creative directions. The dream crystallized his fears about being typecast as a horror writer and the weight of reader expectations.

What struck King most about the dream was its raw emotional truth. While the plot details would evolve during the writing process, the central feeling of powerlessness and the toxic relationship between creator and fan remained unchanged from that original nightmare vision. The dream's premise allowed King to explore themes that had been percolating in his subconscious about the dark side of fandom and the price of literary success.

In "On Writing," King notes that Annie Wilkes emerged from the dream as an amalgamation of his experiences with overzealous fans and his own internal demons. The dream provided not just a plot, but a vehicle to examine the complex relationship between writers and their readers, and the psychological cost of meeting - or defying - audience expectations.

Dream Elements that Influenced the Work

The dream's stark imagery manifested directly in Misery's core elements. The isolated farmhouse setting emerged from the dream's sense of complete separation from the outside world, with King translating that suffocating atmosphere into Paul Sheldon's bedroom prison. The winter storm that cuts off access to Annie's home amplified this isolation, reflecting the dream's feeling of being utterly trapped and dependent on one's captor.

Annie Wilkes' character drew from the dream's representation of toxic fandom personified. Her mood swings between nurturing caretaker and violent tormentor came from the dream's exploration of how admiration can twist into dangerous obsession. The dream showed King how a fan's love for an author's work could become a form of ownership, which he developed into Annie's possessive relationship with both Paul and his characters.

The physical violence in the novel stemmed from the dream's undercurrent of helplessness. Paul's injured state and Annie's infamous hobbling scene represented the dream's theme of a creator being literally crippled by fan expectations. The typewriter became a central symbol, transforming from a tool of creativity into an instrument of torture - mirroring the dream's portrayal of writing as both salvation and imprisonment.

The dream's influence extended to the novel-within-a-novel structure. Paul's forced writing of "Misery's Return" reflected the dream's commentary on artistic compromise. The dream showed King how a writer could become enslaved to their own successful creations, leading to the parallel between Paul's situation and the broader theme of creative bondage.

Through these elements, King expanded his nightmare into a broader examination of the relationship between artists and their audience, the nature of creativity under duress, and the price of commercial success in art.

Turning the Dream into A Novel

The journey from nightmare to novel required King to flesh out the skeletal premise his dream provided. While the core concept of a writer held captive by an obsessed fan emerged fully formed, the process of crafting "Misery" into a complete narrative demanded extensive development.

King faced the immediate challenge of transforming Annie Wilkes from a shadowy dream figure into a three-dimensional character. He drew from his experiences with fans, but also researched the psychology of obsession and mental illness. Annie evolved into a former nurse with a complex history of violence masked by a veneer of folksy charm and religious devotion.

The physical setting required careful consideration to maintain the dream's claustrophobic atmosphere. King chose rural Colorado, using the isolation and harsh winter weather to amplify the sense of confinement. The farmhouse layout, particularly Paul's bedroom-prison, was mapped in detail to ensure consistency throughout the extended cat-and-mouse game between captor and captive.

The dream's premise of forced writing expanded into a deeper exploration of the creative process under duress. King developed the "Misery's Return" storyline as a parallel narrative, showing Paul's desperate attempts to satisfy Annie's demands while secretly plotting his escape. This added layer transformed the simple captivity story into a meditation on the nature of creativity and artistic compromise.

King maintained the dream's psychological horror by grounding the story in physical reality rather than supernatural elements. The violence emerged from human capability rather than mystical forces, making Annie's actions more terrifying through their plausibility. Medical details about Paul's injuries and recovery were meticulously researched to maintain credibility.

The dream served as a springboard rather than a complete blueprint, allowing King to explore themes of addiction, the relationship between artists and their audience, and the price of commercial success. The resulting novel preserved the visceral fear of the original nightmare while expanding into a broader examination of the creative process itself.

Legacy of the Dream

The dream that birthed Misery marked a pivotal moment in King's literary evolution. Moving away from supernatural horror, the novel showcased King's ability to craft tension from purely psychological elements. The claustrophobic terror of Paul Sheldon's captivity proved more chilling than any supernatural monster, demonstrating King's growing mastery of human-centered horror.

Misery's success emboldened King to explore more grounded narratives. The novel's themes of creative imprisonment and toxic fandom surfaced repeatedly in his later works. In "The Dark Half", he further examined the relationship between writers and their creations. "Lisey's Story" delved deeper into the pressures of literary fame and the cost it extracts from both authors and their loved ones.

The dream's influence extended beyond King's writing. Its exploration of fan obsession helped him navigate his own relationship with fame and reader expectations. He became more conscious of maintaining creative freedom while acknowledging his audience's desires, a balance reflected in his willingness to experiment with different genres and styles.

The film adaptation in 1990 amplified the dream's impact. Kathy Bates' Oscar-winning portrayal of Annie Wilkes brought King's nightmare to vivid life, cementing the character in popular culture as the embodiment of obsessive fandom. The movie's success demonstrated how the universal fears captured in King's dream resonated across different mediums.

Throughout his career, King continued to mine his dreams for inspiration, but Misery remained a testament to how a single nightmare could evolve into a work that transcended genre boundaries. The dream's themes of creative bondage, the price of success, and the complex dynamics between artists and audiences became recurring elements in King's literary landscape, influencing not just his horror works but his entire approach to storytelling.

Universal Themes of the Dream

"Misery" connects with readers through primal fears that haunt our collective unconscious. The dream's core elements - being trapped, controlled, and forced to perform under threat - mirror common nightmare scenarios that plague human sleep. Many people experience dreams of confinement or being pursued, making Paul Sheldon's predicament viscerally relatable despite its extreme circumstances.

The power dynamic between Annie and Paul reflects deeper unease about dependency and loss of control. Readers may recognize parallels to situations where they felt powerless - whether in abusive relationships, demanding jobs, or under the thumb of authority figures. Annie's unpredictable shifts between nurturing and violent behavior tap into fears of unstable relationships and the terror of never knowing what might trigger aggression.

The dream's setting - isolation in a remote location during winter - amplifies universal fears of abandonment and helplessness. This resonates with common dreams of being lost or cut off from help, speaking to our fundamental need for connection and safety. The claustrophobic atmosphere of Paul's bedroom-prison echoes nightmares of confinement that many experience.

On a psychological level, the dream explores the terror of being forced to create under duress. This connects to widespread angst about performance pressure and creative blocks. Readers might see reflections of their own experiences with demanding bosses, clients, or audiences who try to control their work. The fear of losing artistic freedom and being forced to produce against one's will strikes a chord with anyone who has felt creatively stifled.

The dream's emphasis on physical vulnerability - particularly through Paul's injuries and dependence on Annie for pain medication - touches on universal fears of bodily harm and medical helplessness. Many people experience nightmares about injury or being at the mercy of caregivers, making these elements deeply resonant.

These universal elements allow readers to process their own fears through the safe distance of fiction while recognizing parts of their own dream experiences in King's nightmare-turned-narrative.

Power of Dreams in Creativity

"Misery" stands as a powerful example of how dreams can unlock creative potential. King transformed a brief nightmare about a deranged fan holding an author captive into a masterwork of psychological horror. The raw emotional impact of his dream - the feelings of helplessness, pain, and creative imprisonment - provided the foundation for the novel's intense atmosphere.

Dreams often distill complex emotions and fears into vivid imagery, and King's ability to expand upon his nightmare demonstrates how these nocturnal visions can evolve into fully realized narratives. The dream's core elements gained deeper meaning through the writing process - Annie Wilkes became more than just a threatening figure, developing into a complex character who embodied obsession, isolation, and the dark side of fandom.

For creative individuals, "Misery's" origin highlights how dreams can bypass conscious limitations and tap into deeper wells of inspiration. The subconscious mind processes experiences and emotions in unique ways during sleep, creating connections and scenarios that might never arise through conscious thought alone. King's transformation of his nightmare into literature shows how artists can harness these dream-born insights.

The novel also illustrates how dreams can reveal personal truths. King's nightmare occurred during a period when he felt pressured by fans' expectations, particularly regarding his fantasy works. The dream crystallized these misgivings into a visceral scenario that allowed him to explore themes of artistic freedom, fan entitlement, and the pressures of success.

Through "Misery", readers gain insight into how dreams can serve as both creative catalyst and psychological mirror. The novel encourages consideration of our own dreams' potential as sources of artistic inspiration and self-discovery, showing how even nightmares can be transformed into meaningful creative works.

Cultural Impact and Significance

"Misery" carved a unique niche in horror literature by stripping away supernatural elements and focusing on human monstrosity. The novel's release in 1987 marked a shift in horror fiction, proving that psychological tension could create more visceral fear than paranormal threats. Bookstores struggled to categorize it - was it horror, psychological thriller, or literary fiction about the creative process?

The book's success spawned numerous imitators in the late 1980s and early 1990s, with publishers seeking similar stories of obsession and confinement. "Misery" helped establish the "fan-gone-wrong" subgenre, influencing works that explored the dark side of celebrity-fan relationships.

The 1990 film adaptation amplified the novel's cultural impact. Kathy Bates' as Annie Wilkes created an iconic screen villain, one whose influence echoes through subsequent portrayals of obsessive characters. The infamous "hobbling" scene entered popular culture as a symbol of visceral horror.

In academic circles, "Misery" sparked discussions about the relationship between authors and their readers, the nature of artistic ownership, and the pressures of commercial success. The novel became required reading in courses examining popular culture and the evolution of horror fiction.

The story's influence extended beyond horror into mainstream literature, showing how genre fiction could tackle serious themes while maintaining commercial appeal. Its examination of creativity under duress resonated with writers and artists, while its exploration of dependency and power dynamics attracted scholarly analysis.

The character of Annie Wilkes became shorthand for toxic fandom, referenced whenever discussions of fan entitlement and creator rights arise. Her impact on popular culture was so significant that the term "number one fan" took on sinister connotations in creative circles.

Shine a Light on the Power of Dreams

"Fill your paper with the breathings of your heart." – William Wordsworth

Unlock the Power of Dreams

Dreams hold incredible power. They spark creativity, reveal hidden truths, and inspire some of the greatest stories ever told. When we share our insights, we help others discover new ideas, new possibilities, and new ways to bring their dreams to life.

Would you help someone just like you—curious about unlocking the inspiration within their dreams but unsure where to start?

Why Your Review Matters

My mission is simple: to help people explore their dreams in a way that's easy, fun, and deeply meaningful. But to reach more dreamers, writers, and visionaries, I need **your help**.

DREAM INSPIRATION IN BOOKS

Most people find books based on reviews. By leaving yours, you're not just sharing your thoughts—you're helping someone else take their first step toward transforming their dreams into stories.

Your review could help...

- One more dreamer find their spark.

- One more writer overcome creative blocks.

- One more storyteller bring their visions to life.

- Omer more person understand the messages within their dreams.

Leaving a review is completely free and takes less than a minute. But the impact? **Endless.**

How to Help

Simply scan the QR code below or visit:

If you love inspiring others, you're my kind of person. Thank you from the bottom of my heart for being part of this journey.

Victor Nyx

References

"Frankenstein" by Mary Shelley

1. Shelley, M. W. (2015). *Frankenstein*. Fingerprint! Publishing.

2. Thorpe, V. (2025, January 21). Frankenstein inspired by suicide of Mary Shelley's half-sister, book reveals. *The Guardian*. https://www.theguardian.com/books/2025/jan/19/frankenstein-inspired-by-suicide-of-mary-shelley-half-sister-fanny-imlay-book-reveals

3. Sampson, F. (2018). *In search of Mary Shelley: The girl who wrote Frankenstein*.

4. Mary Shelley. (2021, May 6). *Biography*. https://www.biography.com/authors-writers/mary-shelley

5. *Hetherington, "Creator and created in Frankenstein."* (n.d.). https://knarf.english.upenn.edu/Articles/hether.html

6. Blakemore, E., & Blakemore, E. (2019, March 12). 'Franken-

stein' was born during a ghastly vacation. HISTORY. https://www.history.com/news/frankenstein-true-story-mary-shelley

7. Shelley, M. (2017). Frankenstein. In *The MIT Press eBooks*. https://doi.org/10.7551/mitpress/10815.001.0001

8. *The Project Gutenberg eBook of Frankenstein: or, The Modern Prometheus, by Mary W. Shelley.* (n.d.). https://www.gutenberg.org/files/42324/42324-h/42324-h.htm

9. Jones, L. (2024, October 21). *What influenced Mary Shelley to write Frankenstein?* TheCollector. https://www.thecollector.com/mary-shelley-wrote-frankenstein-novel/

10. Pass, J. (2024, December 31). *Themes and symbolism in Mary Shelley's Frankenstein — simply put psych.* Simply Put Psych. https://simplyputpsych.co.uk/monday-musings-1/themes-and-symbolism-in-frankenstein

"The Strange Case of Dr. Jekyll and Mr. Hyde" by Robert Louis Stevenson

1. Stevenson, R. (2019). *The strange case of Dr. Jekyll and Mr. Hyde.*

2. *Timeline | Robert Louis Stevenson.* (n.d.). https://robert-louis-stevenson.org/timeline

3. Daiches, D. (1998, July 20). *Robert Louis Stevenson | Biography, famous works, books, death, & Interesting Facts.* Encyclopedia Britannica. https://www.britannica.com/biography/Rob

ert-Louis-Stevenson

4. Rose, P. (2024, August 13). The Wild Adventures of Fanny Stevenson. *The Atlantic*. https://www.theatlantic.com/magazine/archive/2024/09/fanny-robert-louis-stevenson-wife-camille-peri-book/679161/

5. *Treasure Island Author Robert Louis Stevenson Was a Sickly Man with a Robus*. (n.d.). National Endowment for the Humanities. https://www.neh.gov/humanities/2015/julyaugust/feature/treasure-island-author-robert-louis-stevenson-was-sickly-man-robu

6. Byrd, M. (2021, November 17). *Henry and Louis - the American Scholar*. The American Scholar. https://theamericanscholar.org/henry-and-louis/

7. Reporter, G. S. (2017, November 29). Queen of the mixed border. *The Guardian*. https://www.theguardian.com/books/2006/jun/17/featuresreviews.guardianreview7

8. Singh, S., & Chakrabarti, S. (2008). A study in dualism: The strange case of Dr. Jekyll and Mr. Hyde. *Indian Journal of Psychiatry, 50*(3), 221. https://doi.org/10.4103/0019-5545.43624

9. Bell, A. (2022, May 19). *Deacon Brodie, the real life inspiration for Dr Jekyll and Mr Hyde*. Auld Reekie Tours. https://www.auldreekietours.com/2020/08/deacon-brodie-the-real-life-inspiration-for-dr-jekyll-and-mr-hyde/

10. Brown, A. (2019, November 6). Bogeyman and Gentleman:

The Real-Life Dr. Jekyll and Mr. Hyde. *Forbes*. https://www.forbes.com/sites/abrambrown/2019/10/25/bogeyman-and-gentleman-the-real-life-dr-jekyll-and-mr-hyde/

11. *Charles Darwin's Theory of evolution and the intellectual ferment of the mid- and late Victorian periods*. (n.d.). https://www.victorianweb.org/science/darwin/diniejko.html

12. Stevenson, R. L. (n.d.). *A CHAPTER ON DREAMS*. https://rosenbach.org/wp-content/uploads/2024/09/Chapter-on-Dreams-RLS-Scribners-Jan-1888.pdf

"The Call of Cthulhu" by H.P. Lovecraft

1. Lovecraft, H. P. (2016). *The call of Cthulhu*.

2. The Editors of Encyclopaedia Britannica. (1998b, July 20). *H .P. Lovecraft | Biography, Books, & Facts*. Encyclopedia Britannica. https://www.britannica.com/biography/H-P-Lovecraft

3. H.P. Lovecraft. (2020, July 17). *Biography*. https://www.biography.com/authors-writers/hp-lovecraft

4. *The call of Cthulhu*. (n.d.). https://gutenberg.net.au/ebooks15/1500401h.html

5. User, G. (2021, May 11). *Marriage, Failure, and Exile: H.P. Lovecraft in New York — The Gotham Center for New York City History*. The Gotham Center for New York City History. https://www.gothamcenter.org/blog/marriage-failure-and-exile-hp-lovecraft-in-new-york

6. *"The Call of Cthulhu"* by H. P. Lovecraft. (n.d.). https://www.hplovecraft.com/writings/texts/fiction/cc.aspx

7. Johndelaughter. (2015, July 10). *H.P. Lovecraft and H.R. Giger: How Their Dreams Became Our Nightmares.* The Lovecraft eZine. https://lovecraftzine.com/2015/07/10/h-p-lovecraft-and-h-r-giger-how-their-dreams-became-our-nightmares

8. Valjak, D. (2017, June 21). *The influential horror writer H. P. Lovecraft drew inspiration from the nightmares that haunted him throughout his childhood.* Thevintagenews. https://www.thevintagenews.com/2017/03/09/the-influential-horror-writer-h-p-lovecraft-drew-inspiration-from-the-nightmares-that-haunted-him-throughout-his-childhood/

9. Lovecraft, H. (1995). *The dream cycle of H. P. Lovecraft: Dreams of Terror and Death.* National Geographic Books.

10. Sterling, B. (2011, July 4). H. P. Lovecraft's Commonplace Book. *WIRED.* https://www.wired.com/2011/07/h-p-lovecrafts-commonplace-book/

11. *H.P. Lovecraft: Letters to Rheinhart Kleiner.* (n.d.). https://www.hplovecraft.com/writings/sources/lrk.aspx

12. Dickieson, B., & Dickieson, B. (2018, August 23). H.P. Lovecraft's "Supernatural Horror in Literature" - A Pilgrim in Narnia. *A Pilgrim in Narnia - a journey through the imaginative worlds of C.S. Lewis, J.R.R. Tolkien, and the Inklings.* https://apilgriminnarnia.com/2018/08/22/lovecraft-supernatural-horror

DREAM INSPIRATION IN BOOKS

13. *"Quick and Painful": How Call of Cthulhu's scary stories changed roleplaying.* (2020, January 17). Tabletop Gaming. https://www.tabletopgaming.co.uk/features/quick-and-painful-how-call-of-cthulhus-scary-stories-changed-rolepl

14. Thy Horror Cosmic: What is metal's obsession with H.P. Lovecraft? (2024, October 15). *Kerrang!* https://www.kerrang.com/thy-horror-cosmic-celebrating-metals-obsession-with-h-p-lovecraft

"The Shining" by Stephen King

1. King, S. (2013). *The Shining.* Vintage.

2. The Editors of Encyclopaedia Britannica. (2025, January 18). *Stephen King | Biography, books, movies, TV shows, & Facts.* Encyclopedia Britannica. https://www.britannica.com/biography/Stephen-King

3. Brockes, E. (2019, November 25). Stephen King: on alcoholism and returning to the Shining. *The Guardian.* https://www.theguardian.com/books/2013/sep/21/stephen-king-shining-sequel-interview

4. *Stephen King | the author.* (n.d.). https://stephenking.com/the-author

5. Casalena, E., & Casalena, E. (2024, October 1). *5 Beatles songs that appeared in Stephen King Books.* American Songwriter. https://americansongwriter.com/5-beatles-songs-that-appeared-in-stephen-king-books/

6. Hedash, K., Barker, S., & Moser, Z. (2024, September 3). *The Shining: The true story behind the Real-Life Stanley Hotel (Aka the overlook)*. ScreenRant. https://screenrant.com/shining-movie-true-story-stanley-overlook-hotel/

7. Divakaran, S. (2017, June 12). *The Autobiographical Elements in the Shining, by Stephen King*. Rain and a Book. https://rainandabook.wordpress.com/2016/08/24/2889/

8. Wiki, C. T. S. K. (n.d.). *The Stanley Hotel*. Stephen King Wiki. https://stephenking.fandom.com/wiki/The_Stanley_Hotel

9. Beahm, G. W. (1989). *The Stephen King companion*. Andrews McMeel Publishing.

10. Bose, S. D. (2024, September 22). "No arc at all": The reason why Stephen King hated Stanley Kubrick film 'The Shining' *Far Out Magazine*. https://faroutmagazine.co.uk/why-stephen-king-hated-stanley-kubrick-shining/

11. Ferrier, A. (2023, October 30). The origins behind Jack Nicholson's iconic "Here's Johnny!" line from 'The Shining' *Far Out Magazine*. https://faroutmagazine.co.uk/origins-behind-heres-johnny-line-from-the-shining/

"Misery" by Stephen King

1. King, S. (2016). *Misery: A Novel*. Simon and Schuster.

2. King, S. (2010). *On writing: A Memoir of the Craft*. Scribner.

3. Avery, J. (2019, June 18). *Writing and Addiction in Stephen King's MISERY | Book Riot*. BOOK RIOT. https://bookriot.com/writing-and-addiction-in-stephen-kings-misery

4. *Stephen King | Misery*. (n.d.). https://stephenking.com/works/novel/misery.html

5. Shea, L. (n.d.). *Stephen King's Misery Inspired by Dream*. https://lisashea.com/lisabase/dreams/inspirations/misery.html

6. *Misery Journal #5: Conclusion*. (n.d.). https://talkstephenking.blogspot.com/2012/09/misery-journal-5-conclusion.html

7. PrisonerNumber. (n.d.). *The Importance of Imagination: Stephen King's Misery (1987)*. https://www.scriblerusinkspot.com/2019/04/the-importance-of-imagination-stephen.html

8. St Clair, M. (2020, December 8). How Misery Predicted toxic fandom | Features | Roger Ebert. *Roger Ebert*. https://www.rogerebert.com/features/how-misery-predicted-toxic-fandom

9. JoBlo Horror Originals. (2023, December 6). *Misery's Hobbling scene and why it's memorable* [Video]. YouTube. https://www.youtube.com/watch?v=LTnIskKv8B4

www.ingramcontent.com/pod-product-compliance
Lightning Source LLC
Chambersburg PA
CBHW070538030426
42337CB00016B/2250